KU-040-809

ABOUT THE AUTHOR

Simon Hill has done his fair share of losing at backgammon before
going on to play at international level, as a member of the UK team
at the European Championships in Budapest and in the individual
World Championships in Monaco. When not playing backgammon
Simon runs a business, London Place, and lives in London with his
wife, Trish, and their three children.

BACKGAMMON
FOR LOSERS

SIMON HILL

COUPER STREET BOOKS

COUPER STREET BOOKS

First published in 2015 by Couper Street Books

001

Text copyright © Simon Hill, 2015

Diagram copyright © BGLog.org, 2015

Designed and typeset by Couper Street Type Co.

www.couperstreet.com

The moral right of the author has been asserted

ISBN-13: 978-0-9934054-0-2

Set in Arno and AW Conqueror

Printed in the UK

To Dmitri Pavlovich and Jack Wemple

ACKNOWLEDGEMENTS

I am deeply grateful to the following people, who helped make this book better than I imagined it could be. To my editor, Susannah Saary, for giving the book a sound structure and making my words make sense. To my technical editor and mentor/teacher, Phil Simborg, for ensuring I was giving readers the best advice. To Dan Prescott and everyone at Couper Street Books for their publishing expertise. To Simon Woodhead of BGLog for all his painstaking work on the hundreds of essential game illustrations. To Ben Goldsmith, Martin Barkwill, Eric McAlpine and Michael Crane for their support and endorsement. To Chris Lascelles and William Benn for their invaluable advice. I'd also like to thank all my backgammon opponents over the years, winners and losers alike. You learn from every game you play!

CONTENTS

PART I

WHY BACKGAMMON?

*Legendary film director John Huston playing for
high stakes – trying to win back his trousers.*

© John Bryson/Sygma/Corbis

I

CHIMP, CHUMP OR CHAMP?

*'Backgammon – a game that is
ridiculously easy to learn but
ridiculously difficult to master.'*

MICHAEL KONIK

Defeated, I sat in stunned silence for a moment. I had just played possibly the worst backgammon player of all time... and I'd lost. A short time earlier, my opponent – who was called Rupert (or maybe it was Rufus) – had lurched heavily into the room where a dozen other men had been playing backgammon quietly. Breaking the ambient atmosphere with his braying tone, Rupert/Rufus had introduced himself and apologised for keeping me waiting while he'd sneaked in a quick smoke outside. We had been matched against each other in an early round at the famous annual backgammon tournament at White's Club in London. The year before, I'd made it from 64 players down to the last 2, losing in the final to Peter Osborne, a charming but ruthlessly good player. I'd walked away with second prize, a cheque for several thousand pounds, which had paid for plenty more backgammon adventures.

Rupe (or Rufe) had won the dice throw to begin and initially started to move his checkers the wrong way around the board. I'd cringed as I'd pointed this out to him. He was friendly,

Beaten by a buffoon.

and so laid back he was almost horizontal (as the old saying goes). His demeanour had made me rather relaxed, too. And maybe this was my undoing because, to my horror, everything that could have gone wrong did. I went on to lose the match by 2 to 5. Ru made some glaring mistakes, obvious even to me, but time and again the dice rescued him. After he won I kept a fixed grin on my face, like a ventriloquist's dummy, as I congratulated him. He was gracious, almost apologetic, and his kindness made the defeat even more painful; he was frustratingly likeable and I couldn't bring myself to demonise him.

As I ventured out into the cold air, my ego deflating quicker than Ru could light another mini cigar, I

©The Meat and Livestock Commission

© PA/Meat and Livestock Commission

questioned how I could have let this defeat happen? Who was I? The chump who had just lost to a loveable buffoon or the shrewd giant slayer who had climbed to the summit last year?

I've always enjoyed competing. As a kid, I'd been an enthusiastic but untalented games and sports player. It became the family joke. 'I would have won the school junior table-tennis championship if I hadn't been really unlucky in the second round/had a sore elbow/lost my lucky bat,' I would say.

Like many others, as I got older I came to realise that I was never going to be truly excellent at anything. By the time I was in my early 40s, I had long since lost all hope and expectation of ever winning a sporting competition. Reality really kicked in the day I realised I was older than anyone who'd ever won the Wimbledon Men's Singles title. I was, in fact, roughly the same age as the parents of some of the top-seeded players. Whenever I saw an athlete who was enjoying a freakishly long career (like when I watched Ryan Giggs play for Manchester United against Fulham sometime after he'd turned 40), I'd think, 'It's not too late, I could still be really good at *something*', but these hopeful thoughts came to me less and less often, and I started to face the cold, logical fact that I wasn't ever going to come top at anything.

But then I started playing backgammon quite seriously and to my surprise had done really well in a top tournament, playing against good players. That old thought crept back into my head. 'Could I actually get really good at something vaguely sporty?' An old friend of mine, Jamie Lee (who has excelled at shooting and even holds world records) swears that a chimpanzee could, thanks to the luck of the dice in backgammon, win one game in three against a human. If the chimp was playing against Jamie, I have no doubt this would be the case. So had I just been unlucky in my game against Ru or had I been lucky the year before and was I, in reality, not much better than my novice opponent?

As I swayed towards believing that the answer was likely to be more on the chump/chimp end of

Jamie Lee's next opponent?

the scale, I resolved to look into this game more closely. Maybe I wasn't any good, but time was still on my side, and if there was any real skill to be learnt I was determined to give it my best shot.

As I conducted my research into backgammon, I began to believe that no other sport combines luck and skill so deliciously. The extreme reversals of luck and the consequent adrenaline rushes in a match can be thrilling. And yes, I deduced that it was possible to get better and better at it, because although anyone can learn how to play the game in minutes and happily play for years as a beginner without really improving, by following some simple strategies and rules a beginner can become a much stronger player and leave the novice behind. Maybe I'd never be good enough to earn a living at it (like some of the people I met along the way, who regularly win tournaments), but I believed I could learn how to beat most people.

I worked my way through a range of books and played with a few professionals. I played in the London Open and some other tournaments. I even won a few local tournaments. Eventually I played, with a bit of luck, in the World Championships in Monaco (though not *that* much luck... I didn't win it!) After wading through all the books and online forums, however, I never came across a really good, clear book that would give the basic player a better understanding of the game and teach them how to become consistently good at backgammon.

So I decided to write it myself...

Win or lose, what I've learnt is that by following some simple guidelines and strategies, you can beat almost everyone – not top professionals on a sustained basis (this would be too much to ask from a book for novices), but if you apply the rules and strategies in the following chapters, they will enable you to beat most of the players most of the time. You won't win all the time, as I painfully discovered when I faced Ru at that White's tournament, and you won't beat every basic player in a short match, but this book can definitely help you win the majority of the time.

An adrenaline rush from a backgammon match can be almost overwhelming; it's similar to the kind of buzz that many people chase by motor racing, swimming with sharks or skydiving. Trust me, I've tried all of these things in the past and can vouch for the fact that backgammon produces exactly the same kind of chemical reactions and can easily give you a thrill-filled ride on the adrenaline roller-coaster.

It's true that you or I would be more likely to beat a great player over 1 game than over 50, but anything's possible. Unlike chess (which is all skill with no luck involved) or roulette (which is 100% luck), backgammon is a tantalizing mixture of skill and luck... in the short term, at least; in the long term, the good and bad luck cancels itself out and

Picture courtesy of http://mygopengresort.com/

Almost as good as winning a gammon…

it all comes down to skill. No other game combines luck and skill in quite the same way as backgammon does. That's why it's so easy to learn to be better than almost everyone you know.

In the following chapters, first we're going to look back at the history of the game and some of its great players, and then we will go through the basics of play, some tactics and how to think about the numbers. We will also talk about the importance of having a game plan, how to play openings and reply to them, how to approach the middle of a game, and how to play the end stages. We will then look at doubling, run through some great backgammon tips and laws, think about different types of tournament and talk a little about computer play. Finally, we will reflect on some parallels between life and backgammon, and discuss the next steps you can take to improve your game.

I was going to call this book *Backgammon for Life*, then one day my son, Teddy, asked me how I was getting on with writing *Backgammon for Losers*. I felt his twist on my original title really nailed the point of the book. Only my goal is to equip you with all the knowledge you need to move from being a loser to being a winner.

Who wants to be a chump when even a chimp could learn to be a champ?

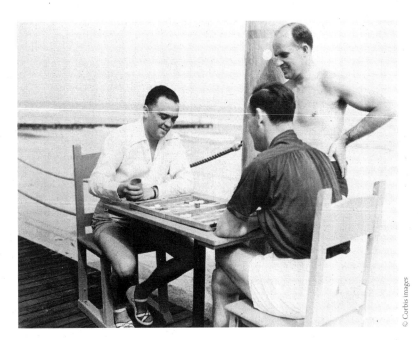

FBI Director J Edgar Hoover is wearing his lucky shoes…

© Corbis images

2

BACKGAMMON
BACKSTORY

*Backgammon is an ancient and fascinating
game that requires both luck and skill –
luck keeps the game interesting,
but skill will always be rewarded.*

PAUL MAGRIEL
(FORMER BACKGAMMON WORLD CHAMPION)

BACK IN THE NERVOUS NINETIES...

I remember watching a tense football match between England and Germany. It was the Euro '96 Championships. England was hosting the competition and we had made it into the semi-final to play against Germany. I had watched most of the games with friends, but found myself watching the semi-final on my own. My flatmate was away so I was blissfully alone. Feet up, full of pizza, using the empty box as an ashtray, I watched England score early on and then Germany equalise. There followed a war of attrition that led to extra time and, ultimately, penalties. I felt absurdly stressed and excited by this game, drawn in to the point that nothing else mattered, so nervous watching the penalties that I felt sick. And yet I was struck by how odd it was that I got so emotionally involved. I'm not a big football fan (I didn't know the names of all of the England players, never mind the Germans) and although I was keen on the game at school, I really wasn't any good. I kept telling myself that it was only a game, yet I was perched on the edge of my chair, about to throw up with nerves (I swear, it wasn't the pizza!) The thrill of the penalty shoot-out was overwhelming. Of course, England lost 6-5 on penalties and Germany went on to win the tournament... and life went on.

Photo: BBC

Penalty agony.

The next time I felt that sick with excitement was some years later during a backgammon match. The feeling was even more intensified because I was in the game, not just a spectator. It was like I was on the pitch taking that penalty kick, just me against the goalkeeper. Nothing else in the world mattered in that thrilling moment. As I played more and more big matches, I found I regularly felt this level of adrenalin.

I can understand why backgammon has survived and evolved for thousands of years, and why players have been captivated by it!

We know the game was played in ancient Rome as it's depicted on a painting in Pompeii and there is reference to the Emperor Nero playing the game for the equivalent of £10,000 per point (presumably everyone had to let him win). King Tutankhamen even had some boards and dice buried with him, which proves that the Egyptians were playing backgammon over three thousand years ago, at a time when some Europeans were still chasing their lunch with a spear. In fact, the Egyptians invented a mechanical dice box that threw the dice onto the table automatically, thus ensuring you couldn't cheat.

There are references to back-gammon being played in Britain dating back more than 600 years; Chaucer mentioned backgammon in *The Canterbury Tales* and the poet Samuel Butler wrote about the game during the 17th century. In the USA, Thomas Jefferson found the time to record his backgammon losses in a journal he wrote in 1776, just three weeks before he drafted the Declaration of Independence. The game took its biggest leap

Playing backgammon in the 17th century – before smoking was banned in pubs.

forward in 1925, when someone invented the concept of doubling (doubling the stakes of a game during the course of play). While most people think it was the Grand Duke Dmitri Pavlovich who first came up with doubling, a few think it might have been Jack Wemple. I like to think that Grand Duke Dmitri was responsible because he has the more colourful story, having been credited for taking part in the murder of the Russian monk, Rasputin, as well as assisting Coco Chanel in cooking up her No.5 perfume.

The Grand Duke presumably explaining doubling to Coco Chanel, or maybe he's suggesting changing the No.5 recipe. Either way, she doesn't look convinced.

Doubling created the rich and fascinating game that we play today; it changed backgammon fundamentally and forever.

Since the introduction of doubling in the 1920s, people have found that by combining the skill of moving the counters around the board (known as checker play) with the art – and it *is* an art – of using the doubling cube, a player can become seriously hard to beat. No player can become great without mastering both of these abilities.

The game gradually grew in stature through the 20th century. Winston Churchill recommended it to the Fourth Sea Lord as being better than card games for the Navy during the Second World War, saying, 'I have no doubt it would amuse the sailors'.

Backgammon became even more glamorous and fashionable in the 1970s; it was almost as popular as Charlie's Angels, Billie Jean King and flares. Perhaps this was because of the rise of global tournaments. Prince Alexis Obolensky held the first global tournament in the Bahamas in 1964. Later, the World Championships were held in Monaco, where they are still played today. (A Prince? The Bahamas? Monaco? It's no wonder backgammon started to look glamorous!)

Many of the best books on the game were written in the 1970s by the top players of the time, and although some examples of play have since been proven by computer technology to be inaccurate, a few of these books have aged well and remain sound in terms of their thinking behind the game.

The 1970s – when fashion and backgammon collided.

Conversely, others are quite hard to follow and some read as if they were knocked out in haste to cash in on the backgammon wave. Confusingly, many of these books have the same snappy title (simply, *Backgammon*).

Some great players emerged in the 1970s, such as the world champion, Paul Magriel, who wrote the best book of this era (called... you guessed it... *Backgammon*) in 1973.

A couple of thrilling pages from one of the books written in the 1970s.

The players John Crawford and Oswald Jacoby not only wrote books together (coming up with the slightly more creative title, *The Backgammon Book*, for one of them) but they also each managed to have a backgammon rule named after them.

And then came the 70s… When you could smoke and drink a can of Tab at the table.

The better books were written with expert players in mind and the examples are very complex. This is useful at an advanced level but for most players I advise not trying to run before you can walk. It's important to get the fundamentals right – playing the right strategies and avoiding making major blunders – before moving on to the finer points of the game. That's why I'm keeping this book quite straightforward; it probably won't turn you into the next world champion, but it should help you to move from being a loser to being a winner… at least in backgammon!

Live and let dice? Doubles are forever? I like my dice shaken?

3

THE GIANTS OF
THE GAME

*The way to become a good player is to learn to
make good moves. If you make better moves
than your opponents, you will win in the long run.
But in the short run, there are no guarantees.*

BILL ROBERTIE
(TWO TIMES BACKGAMMON WORLD CHAMPION)

MEETING THE BIG CHAMP

As I wandered through the playing hall at the World Championships at the Fairmont Hotel in Monaco I calculated that there must have been close to 40 backgammon matches going on, but one clearly stood out from the rest: there was a big swarm of people around the table. It was clearly a big match and one of the competitors was clearly... well... big!

The big man was Falafel Natanzon (known simply as Falafel). Falafel's opponent looked nervous; I watched him spill a pint of orange juice all over the table. Falafel has that effect on people; he is disarmingly brilliant. He's an intuitive player who came from nowhere to dominate the world of backgammon in only a few short years. After a game, Falafel's demeanour always changes; he is friendly and quick-witted, and ready to talk to anyone about the game he's just played (and won). Falafel is globally recognised as a fearsome competitor and consistently ranks in the top three in the world. He explains his passion, saying, 'I used to play chess until I discovered backgammon. I instantly fell in love with the game, and have been totally consumed and obsessed with it ever since. I play, practice, review and analyse, and I'm always looking to learn something new.'

Above: Falafel…
Left: Mochy (after winning the Munich Open in 2014)

Many backgammon players love to gamble and not exclusively on the game! Falafel and the great Japanese player Masayuki Mochizuki (known as Mochy) reportedly had a $1 million bet with a wealthy German businessman that the two of them could become the same weight through Falafel dieting and Mochy increasing his calorie intake (Mochy weighed about half as much as Falafel at the time of the bet). It's rumoured that the players won the bet... and shortly after, resumed their original shapes!

Most people think of backgammon, if they think of it at all, as a game for high-rollers that's cooler than chess or bridge. In the film *Octopussy*, James Bond did not take on the suave baddie Kamal Khan at chess or challenge him to a race to finish the *Telegraph* jumbo crossword... they played backgammon. But is the glamorous label justified? Well, yes and no. Backgammon is definitely more exciting than chess because of the element of luck. In a short match, anyone is in with a chance if they know the basic moves. However, at its highest level the game demands just as much from your intellect as chess. Backgammon tournaments don't look so different from chess tournaments, they are just much louder.

THE GIANTS OF BACKGAMMON

Every sport has a hall of fame, and backgammon is no exception. As with all other sports, there is an illustrious list of backgammon giants. Every two years the best players and tournament directors in the world are asked which players they most respect in their peer group. From their answers, a list of the top 64 players in the world is compiled (the number reflecting the 64 on the doubling cube).

Right, top: Akiko Yazawa (2014 world champion)
Right: Nack Ballard (Arguably the world's greatest ever backgammon player. Nack has even invented his own version of the game. Naturally he called it Nackgammon!)

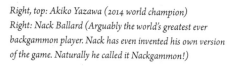

BACKGAMMON GIANTS: THE ALL-TIME BEST

Player	Country	Rating									Total Points
		1993	1995	1997	1999	2001	2003	2005	2007	2009	
Nack Ballard	USA	7	4	3	2	1	1	1	2	6	270
Neil Kazaross	USA	17	10	6	4	7	7	2	5	3	236
Paul Magriel	USA	4	5	5	5	6	5	10	12	-	212
Kit Woolsey	USA	9	12	8	10	10	11	5	8	13	211
Mike Senkiewicz	USA	2	1	2	6	8	16	19	18	32	193
Bill Robertie	USA	6	9	10	15	14	15	20	17	26	165
Mike Svobodny	USA	5	7	4	9	12	19	24			151
Jerry Grandell	Sweden			9	1	2	2	9			142
Falafel Natanzon	Israel					17	8	4	1	2	133
Peter Jes Thomsen	Denmark		25	17	20	13	17	12	11	24	125
Jake Jacobs	USA			25	14	9	12	14	14	19	124

Some of these players become famous within the international backgammon community and many appear on the list year in, year out. Falafel has appeared on the list consistently in recent years. Then there is US player, Nack Ballard, who has even invented his own version of the game. The top Japanese players include Mochy and Akiko Yazawa, the 2014 World Champion. Akiko is only the third Japanese player to win the world championship and the fourth ever female winner.

Kit Woolsey, Bill Robertie, Paul Magriel and Neil Kazaross are all long-standing big names from the USA – traditionally the country that has produced many of the top players, although with the game's popularity rising, Japan and Denmark have also emerged as strong nations. Some of the main tournaments are held in these countries; there are numerous tournaments in the USA, and there is the Japan Open and the Nordic Open.

Tim Holland… dressed like a dirty rotten scoundrel.

Nack Ballard has compiled a table of the lists of the backgammon giants from the last two decades, at the top of which is... Nack Ballard!

Bill Robertie won the world championship twice in the 1980s and wrote a number of backgammon books including one called *Backgammon for Winners* (there goes my sequel title!)

Only one player has won the world championship three times; the USA's Tim Holland, who first won the tournament when it was held in Las Vegas in the 1960s. Given the fierce competition these days, and the many professional-level players, it seems statistically unlikely that anyone will ever achieve this hat-trick again.

Tim Holland was something of a golf hustler in the 1950s. When he discovered that the older, richer members of his club were playing backgammon, he quickly got involved. Apparently he lost $30,000 as he was learning the ropes, but by the 1970s he was making $60,000 a year from the game and gained a reputation as a very cool customer. John Bradshaw recalls, 'He did not speak, he did not smile; his eyes rarely left the table.'

We may wonder what all these great players have in common. As far as I can see, there are two common threads. Firstly, and not surprisingly, they are all rather good at mathematics. Secondly, they have spent an immeasurable number of hours playing and studying the game. In his excellent book *Outliers*, Malcolm Gladwell explores the theory that to be superbly good at anything you will need to spend more than 10,000 hours doing it. He applies the theory to the Beatles, Michael Jordan and Bill Gates. I believe you could also apply it to the leading backgammon players.

WORK, REST AND PLAY

In recent times, some of the great players have gone to extremes to improve their game. Matt Cohn-Geier, one of the greats in the modern game, became a giant only four years after he took up backgammon, a unique feat that is rather encouraging for the rest of us. Matt, who is one of the youngest top professionals, spent his college years playing backgammon for many hours a day. He says, 'Early on, I spent my spare time getting drunk and playing chess. Later, I spent it getting drunk and playing backgammon. Still later, I gave up drinking altogether and just spent it playing backgammon.'

Young giant Matt Cohn-Geier

Malcolm Davis, probably writing a cheque to buy even more servers.

Malcolm Davis has won many tournaments in the US and has had books written about his matches; he spends a huge amount of time learning how to play better. In the basement of his house he runs a collection of computer servers running different rollouts and match situations; it helps to be this obsessive if you want to get to the top. Malcolm has placed first or second in a major tournament 75 times in the past 40 years.

According to Mochy, 'If you want to be among the top ten players in the world, you have to do a lot more work. You should devote *all* of your time and life to the game for at least a few years. Backgammon is a difficult game; we are not sure how to play some of the opening rolls, even though this game has a history of 5000 years.' He goes on to admit, 'I have just kept studying, playing, reading and thinking about the game every day, for years and years. I must admit

Photo Copyright by Kathy Liberopoulos

that I'm lazy and I compromised a lot in my life, but never in backgammon. I spend a lot of time not just playing backgammon, but studying and teaching, as well. I am not sure exactly how many hours per week, but most of my waking hours are spent in backgammon activities.'

Neil Kazaross says, 'The best way to improve at backgammon is to get your hands dirty and really work to learn to understand this game,' while Paul Magriel simply states, 'The best way to learn backgammon is to play it.'

A tale of two very different shirts: Falafel and Mochy receive awards from Yamin Yamin, who compiles the Giants of Backgammon list every two years.

Many of the top backgammon players find that their family life suffers as a result of their obsession. Divorce is endemic amongst those who are playing at the highest levels. Phil Simborg once said, 'I have never let any of my marriages interfere with my backgammon.'

Obviously I'm not trying to encourage you to get so obsessive about the game that you sacrifice your marriage (unless that is a desirable goal for you!) This book isn't about making it hard work, it's about learning how to play good backgammon whilst keeping it fun. Backgammon is the best way I know to compete fiercely whilst still (as Andy Roddick put it, while being thrashed 6-3, 6-1 by Andy Murray at the Queen's Club tennis tournament) 'keeping it social.' Initially and most importantly, it's about learning how to play smart enough to beat just about everyone you know, most of the time.

PART II

HOW TO PLAY

Hugh Hefner not focusing on his game.

©HughHefner/Twitter

4

TOOLS &
RULES

*One of the fascinating things about backgammon
is that at first it all seems so clear, almost simple.
I think any intelligent person could master
half of the game in a week. But the rest of it?
I know brilliant players who have been playing
it for years, and they admit that to this day there are
parts of the game they don't fully understand.*

HUGH HEFNER

O ne of the earlier tournaments I played was the annual charity event at the RAC club in London. I had rattled through the first two rounds. Both players were clearly better than me and more experienced at tournament play, but they couldn't seem to buy a good throw that day.

Fortunately for me, the matches were only to 5 points. At one point, in one of my games, I took an absurd risk, but it paid off. I knew how risky my move was when I saw the stunned look on my opponent's face; it was the unmistakable look of someone being trounced by a less experienced and generally inferior player.

In the third round I came across a young player called Yan Kit Chan. Quietly spoken, Yan explained to me that he needed me to tell him the outcome of each roll of the dice, and where I had moved my pieces... because he was completely blind.

Yan has learnt to play backgammon even though he has never seen a board. He has grown into an exceptionally strong player and regularly does well in tournaments in the UK and the US. I was in awe of the fact that he was able to picture the entire match in his head; he knew the positions of all 30 checkers at any given point in the game. He would move his pieces by carefully feeling them amongst the other checkers on the board. He always knew where

Yan Kit Chan collecting a trophy.

every checker was positioned. At one point he even corrected me when I miscounted one of my moves. Behind his softly spoken manner and gentle charm I could see a steely determination. If Yan can apply himself and become a superb player, so can anyone.

Although backgammon is a complex game in all its possibilities, the basic elements can be learned quickly (which is more than can be said for bridge or mah-jongg... or studying horseracing form!) In backgammon, you can become a good player in a fairly short space of time. After that you might choose to read some rather more technical books, play stronger players, play people online and maybe even get a good computer program to play against in order to improve. Or you might just be happy beating your friends and leaving them scratching their heads, baffled as to how you did it.

My aim is to help you move from being a beginner, or a basic player, through to being good enough to beat nine out of ten of your friends, while remembering not to play the tenth guy for money.

THE TOOLS

The equipment you need to play backgammon consists of:

A backgammon board

30 checkers. That's 15 each of two different colours for each of the two players. (In this book, the checkers are black and white. In every example shown, you are White and your opponent is Black.)

A pair of dice each

A dice shaker each

One larger dice, used for offering doubles,
known as **the cube**.

THE OBJECT OF THE GAME

Backgammon is a race between two players. Each player moves his 15 pieces (checkers) around the board, and then starts to remove them, which is known as **bearing off**. The first player to bear off all his checkers is the winner; all you have to do to win a game of backgammon is bear off all your pieces first.

THE BACKGAMMON BOARD

Here's an image of the board in the style we are going to use throughout this book. The white arrow indicates the direction that you, as the White player, will be racing. The Black arrow shows the direction that your opponent will move in the opposite direction. The board is divided into four equal parts with six triangles (points), alternately coloured dark and light, in each quarter; this gives you a total of 24 points.

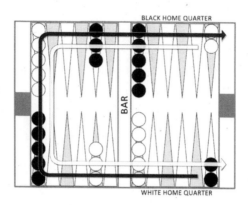

The bar runs down the middle of the board and is where your checkers are placed when your opponent's checker lands on it, which is known as being **hit**.

Your side of the board (which is the bottom half in all of the diagrams) is split into your **outer board** on the left and your **home board** on the right.

Your home board is the final destination for your checkers, as you can see from the white arrow. The opposite side of the board consists of your opponent's home board and outer board; these mirror your own.

You always start with the same layout of checkers, but depending on which side you are sitting they either move **anticlockwise** (finishing in the bottom right quarter) or **clockwise** (finishing in the bottom left quarter), so make sure you get used to playing both clockwise and anticlockwise. Every time you are moving your checkers clockwise, your opponent is playing anticlockwise, and vice versa.

In all examples where I've shown an image of the board, you are White and your opponent is Black so in this book your checkers are moving anti-clockwise. (I will be referring to White as 'you' and to Black as 'he'; this is not meant to imply that backgammon is only a game for men. In fact, the current world champion is a woman.)

Here is the opposite view of how the board looks to your opponent, Black, who is moving his checkers clockwise:

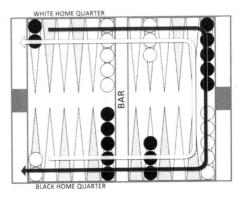

An upside-down view. How the board looks from where your opponent (who is moving his counters clockwise) is sitting.

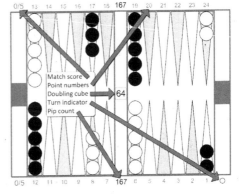

The arrows in the diagram to the right point to some of the other standard features you will find in the diagrams in this book:

Throughout, the value of the dice will be shown using the '+' sign, so if a player throws a 6 and a 5, it will be shown as **6+5**.

The **match score** is shown on the top and bottom left; in this case both players are still on 0 in a game to 5 points.

Standard features in the diagrams shown.

Around the board the **points are numbered** from 1 to 24, which will help you to locate the position of the checkers I am referring to.

In the middle of the bar rests the **doubling cube**, which always shows 64 at the start of each game (as shown in the above diagram).

On the top or bottom right is the **turn indicator**; this indicates which player's turn it is. In the diagram shown above, it is White's turn, as marked with a White circle on your side of the board.

Finally, each player's **pip count** is shown in the middle of his side of the board. Your pip count is the exact number of moves it would take you to move all of your checkers off the board. The arrow in the diagram above points to 167, which is always your starting pip count. Your pip count goes down as you move your checkers around the board, and goes up when you are hit and have to move a checker around the board from the beginning again.

HITTING

When a player only has one checker on a point (known as a **blot**), his opponent can **hit** it. (You cannot land on a point with two or more of your opponent's checkers on it, only on empty points or a point with a blot on it). When a checker is hit, it is taken off the board and placed on the bar in the middle of the board.

RE-ENTERING

On the next turn of the player who's been hit, he must **re-enter** the hit checker from the bar and start at the beginning back in his home quarter; that is, as long as he can throw a number that will land him on an empty or single-checker-occupied point. He cannot re-enter if the points that correspond with the values on his dice are blocked by his opponent's checkers. (This is actually a tactic that will be explained in a later chapter). So you must throw a number that gets you back onto the board, and you have to re-enter your checker on the bar before you can continue your turn and move any of your other checkers on the board.

Simon Woodhead from BGlog.org, who designed the excellent diagrams in this book, has a great way of explaining being hit in backgammon to beginners; he says it's very much like when you are playing *Snakes & Ladders* and you land on a snake that takes you back to the start.

It can take a number of throws to get the right dice to re-enter. While you are waiting to re-enter a checker into the game you are said to be **dancing on the bar!**

Dancing on the bar... not always as fun as it looks.

ROLLING TO START

Each player rolls one dice to determine who starts. The player who gets the highest value goes first, but *must* play the dice on the board. If you win the roll, you play your single dice and your opponent's single dice as your opening move. You can't roll both of your own dice again and hope for something better.

If you both throw the same number, you roll again.

SHAKING THE DICE

I was pretty surprised to learn that there are different rules in various different countries and tournaments about how you must shake your dice. As a rule of thumb try to make sure that you shake your shaker **three times** before releasing the dice and that you **release the dice properly** from the shaker so that they roll across the board a short distance before coming to rest, rather than just letting them 'plop out'.

COCKED DICE

If either dice lands on top of a checker, or at an angle (leaning against a checker or the side of the board), it is known as a **cocked dice** and both dice must be thrown again. It's no crime to throw cocked dice, even the top players do it frequently, so don't worry about it, just throw again.

Your dice must also **land in the right-hand half** of the board (as you are looking at it). If one of your dice jumps into the left-hand half, it is usually considered to be cocked dice and you will have to throw again.

MOVING YOUR CHECKERS AROUND THE BOARD

On each turn you move the checkers around the board the number of moves that are shown on your dice. You can move any combination of the numbers that you throw unless you're **blocked** from doing so by your opponent's checkers (you cannot land on a point that has two or more of your opponent's checkers on it). If you can't move at all (perhaps because you are on the bar and haven't thrown a value that allows you to re-enter), then you miss your turn. This happens surprisingly often, mostly later in the game after your opponent has built a strong home board. If you can only play one of the numbers then you *must* move that one and forgo the second.

Be careful that you don't automatically combine the total of the two dice to work out how many spaces to move. Throwing 4+1 does not mean you necessarily have to move 5 consecutive spaces with one single checker (although you can if that is your best move). This is especially important to remember if a 5 would block you from moving or re-entering after being hit. You can always move one checker a 1 or a 5 and then take the remaining moves with a different checker.

Always keep the number on each dice separate in your mind.

When you roll a double you can move each number of each dice twice: i.e. you get 4 x the value of the double you've thrown. This is usually a nice boost in your game!

BEARING OFF

To finish and win the game, all your checkers must come off the board. You can't begin to bear checkers off until all your checkers are in your home board. You *can*, however, bear off regardless of where your opponent's checkers are.

Once all your checkers are in your home board, you roll the dice and bear off checkers in moves that match the numbers you roll. If you roll a number and can't bear off because

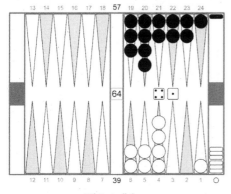

White strolls home.

the number on your dice is lower than the number of moves it would take to bear off your checker, you must **move a checker** the number of moves shown. If you're hit while bearing off you must re-enter that checker and get it back into your home board before you can start bearing off again. This happens more often than you'd think.

In the example on the left, you are heading for a win, having already borne off six checkers, while Black has only borne off one. Your current throw of 4+1 means you can bear off another two checkers (the checker on your 1-point and a checker from your 4-point).

THE CUBE

The large dice in the middle of the bar is known as **the cube** and has the values 2, 4, 8, 16, 32 and 64 painted on each of its six sides. The cube is not thrown, it is used to signify the offering of a double and keeps track of the stakes in a game as they increase. Once the first player offers a double, the player who accepts the double places the cube, showing the number of points that the game is now worth, on their side of the bar. That player is now the only one who can offer to double the points again. So the cube also shows which player holds the right to double. When you offer your opponent a double, you are offering to play the game for double the original points that were being played for (having started the game playing for one point).

 A player can offer a double only when it is his turn and before he throws his dice. After the initial double is offered, only the player who has accepted the last double, and therefore controls the cube, can offer the next double. If his opponent accepts the next double, the cube is turned to its next higher value and is placed on the side of bar closest to the player who has accepted the double. This player then becomes the new owner of the cube and is the only player who can offer a subsequent double. And so on. After that first double is accepted, think of it like a game of tennis; you can only offer a double when the ball (i.e. the cube) is in your court.

Until the first double is offered, the cube sits in the middle of the bar with the value 64 facing up.

DOUBLING RULES

At any point in the game, a player can offer his opponent a double before he throws his dice. The player who is offered the double (the cube) can choose to accept it and play the game for double the points, or to decline it and forfeit the game, so the player who offered the double wins the number of points the game was being played for at that point. It's very similar to making a bet in poker: if you like your odds of winning, you want to raise the stakes. In backgammon, if you are ahead by a significant margin, you want to either play for more points or force your opponent to quit so that you get the points that are being played for at that stage in the game before your luck changes!

Usually no more than two or three doubles are offered and accepted within one game, and games are sometimes played without any doubles being offered.

GAMMONS AND BACKGAMMONS

A normal game (without any doubles being offered) wins or loses a single point. A **gammon** is when the losing player has failed to bear off any checkers by the time the other player has won. When you are gammoned you lose twice the stake (so, two points if no doubles have been offered, four points if you had been playing for two points, eight points if the game was being played for four points, and so on.)

A **backgammon** is when you lose without bearing off any checkers *and* you still have one or more checkers in your opponent's home board or on the bar. When you are backgammoned you lose three times the stake. This doesn't happen very often but it's very painful when it does!

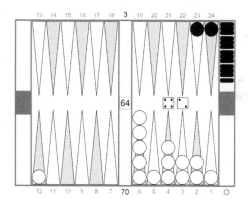

White is gammonned.

In the example above we can see that Black is certain to finish with his next throw (because the lowest he can throw is 1+2, which will take his remaining two checkers off the board). Although you (White) throw a 4+2, which is enough to land the final checker in your home board, it's not enough to avoid a gammon because you haven't managed to bear off any checkers. It's close, but you still lose double the stakes.

Master of comic timing Charlie Chaplin with
Paulette Goddard on Charlie's yacht, 1933.

5

PLAYING
THE GAME

Life to me is the greatest of all games.
The danger lies in treating it as a trivial game,
a game to be taken lightly, and a game
in which the rules don't matter much.
The rules matter a great deal.

JON M HUNTSMAN SR.

t*akes more than just knowing the rules. At the 2014 World Championships in Monaco, I faced a professional player from Japan who didn't speak much English. Half way through our first game, he stood up from the table, went to find the match referee and had a long conversation with the guy. I didn't know what was going on until the referee walked over and informed me that my opponent had reported me for not shaking three times every time I threw the dice. I had no idea that this was against the rules, in this particular tournament at least. Fortunately, the match referee let me off with a warning but I made a mental note to check out the local rules at subsequent competitions.*

I was lucky enough to beat the Japanese rule stickler. I must admit, I felt a twinge of sympathy for the poor bloke who had flown half way around the world only to be knocked out 18 to 17 by a nervous, fidgety Brit who couldn't even throw the dice properly! But I did wonder if his reporting of me had been a little bit of gamesmanship with the intention of throwing me off course – which, for a while, it did.

◎

Let's take another look at the board as it is at the start of each game and go through some of the terms used in the game, as well as studying some of the fundamental positions, to help you to start thinking more strategically about your game.

BACKMARKERS AND MIDMARKERS

Throughout this book we will refer to those counters furthest behind in the race as the **backmarkers**. In the illustration below, which shows the position of all the checkers before the game starts, you have two backmarkers on your 24-point.

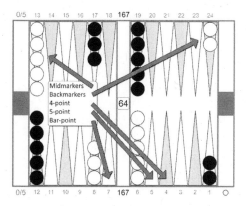

Some key positions and terms.

Midmarkers are those checkers that are half way around the board. You start the game with five midmarkers on your 13-point.

5-POINT, 4-POINT AND BAR-POINT

The crucial points that you should become familiar with are your **5-point**, **4-point** and **bar-point** (your 7-point, often referred to as the bar-point because it is alongside the bar.) These three points, on both sides of the board, are crucial strategic territory over which the players fight. Whoever wins the fight is often in a winning position from that stage in the game.

MAKING A POINT

A **point** (not to be confused with the named triangles, 4-point, 5-point, etc.) is made when you have placed two or more checkers on one of your point positions, which means that your opponent is blocked from landing on it.

MAKING A PRIME

You make a **prime** when you have two or more consecutive points in a row. If you have two in a row, you have a 2-point-prime, if you have 3 in a row you have a 3-point-prime, etc. (Again, do not be confused with point positions here; a 2-point-prime is not referring to your 2-point position. A 2-point-prime could be on your 4-point and 5-point positions.)

The ultimate prime is a **6-point-prime**. If your opponent has one or more checkers stuck behind a 6-point-prime, he can't move them at all until you vacate on of the points and break up the blockade. Even if your opponent throws 4+5 to make a total of 9, he cannot simply move 9 spaces and jump over a prime because he can't land the 4 or 5 move on one of your points in the prime (this shows, again, how you must always think in terms of the *two* moves shown by the values on the dice and not automatically combine them). The more primes (consecutive points) you have, the better. There is no need to create a prime longer than a 6-point-prime, because your 6-point-prime is already impenetrable.

In the example below, you (White) have created a 5-point-prime, almost trapping 2 of Black's checkers behind it. Black has only managed to make a 2-point-prime on his 5-point and 6-point positions. In this example, you are in a better position than Black and are therefore more likely to win the game.

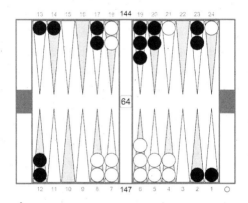

White has created a 5-point-prime.

BLOTS

Having a blot – an exposed checker – on the board is not as bad as many beginners assume it is.

Sometimes you will be forced to leave a blot (known as a **forced blot**) because the number of spaces you must move will force you to leave a single checker exposed at the end of your turn. However, you might have a choice as to *where* to leave a forced blot. You should weigh up the advantage of leaving it in a position where it is least likely to get hit, against leaving it in a position where you can best use it as long as it doesn't get hit. You might strategically leave a blot in a position where it would be painful for your opponent to hit you because it would force him to give up a valuable point that he is holding.

Whenever I see a player being really tidy with their checkers, avoiding leaving checkers exposed to being hit, I know from early on in the game that they are likely to be heading for failure. Whole games without anyone leaving blots, and with no one getting hit, are extremely rare. In the early stages of the game, your opponent hasn't had a chance to create a good prime, so if you do get hit you're unlikely to be blocked from re-entering the board; you can soon get back in the race and it's no big loss. Don't be afraid of hitting and being hit in the early stages of the game.

SLOTTING

Slotting simply means leaving a strategic blot in the hope that you'll be able to cover it with a second checker, to create a point, before your opponent hits you. **You can purposely create a blot by landing a checker on an empty point, or by leaving one exposed after moving a checker that had been part of a duo on an existing point.** The best places to do this are the places where it is most advantageous to make a point (for example your 5-point or your opponent's 5-point).

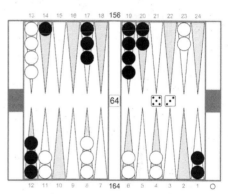

White is forced to leave a blot.

In the example on the right, you have rolled a 5+3 so you are going to be forced to leave at least one blot. You have a number of options, including the opportunity to slot your 5-point (as shown in the diagram bottom, right). If you are lucky and Black does not hit this blot on his next throw, there are several combinations of the dice that will give you the 3, 6 or 8 that will allow you to make the 5-point. If you *do* manage to make that 5-point, it will be nestled neatly between the 6-point and the 4-point, thus making a strong 3-point-prime. This will make it harder for Black to free his backmarkers.

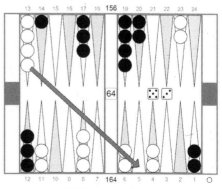

Slotting your 5-point.

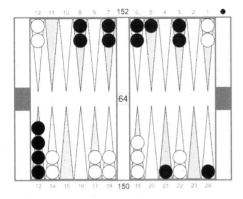

Black has more blots but a better board overall.

Even though creating a blot leaves a checker vulnerable for a while, slotting is often the first step in building a point. You have the opportunity to cover that blot with a second checker and thus create a point.

In the example above, Black has three blots. White doesn't have any blots so looks to be in a safer position. However, Black is a clear favourite to win this game because it's his throw and he has already slotted points in both your home quarter and his own home quarter. This could boost his potential to create strong positions further down the line.

Making blots does involve risk but if done effectively it shows that you are thinking ahead and trading some present risk for creating a good future position.

BUILDERS

A **builder** can be either a single checker on a strategic point position (i.e. a blot that you have purposely slotted), or a third checker that is placed on a point that is already securely occupied by two checkers. In the latter case, you are parking your checker on an existing point in the hope that you can soon use it to create a new point and *build a stronger position*. Any checkers over and above the first two that are used to create a point are surplus to requirements and are therefore useful **builders**. Creating builders shows that you are planning well for the future stages of the game. And, as we've already discussed, leaving exposed blots that could be hit by your opponent is not as risky as you might think, especially in the early stages of the game. Again, very few games run their course without a number of hits taking place. However, it is preferable to be hit fairly early on in the game; being hit later in the game, when your opponent has had the opportunity to build up a strong prime, is more of a problem.

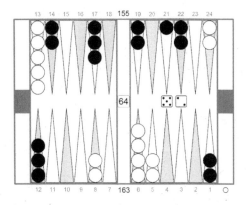

With the 5+2 throw, you can leave two builders: move a third checker onto your 8-point and then slot your 11-point or 4-point.

In the diagram above you have thrown a 5+2. For your 5-move, it's obvious that moving a checker from your group of checkers at the midpoint (your 13-point, which is the halfway point around the board) to land on your 8-point position (where you already have a point) is a safe way to progress and there are no other reasonable alternatives. This leaves you a builder for the future.

Now for your 2-move. You can't play a checker into a safe position, but you could slot your 4-point in your home board or your 11-point in your outer board. Generally the 11-point is a better option because you have less chance of being hit and more chance of building a prime and blocking Black.

Shown below are your two optimal moves for your 5+2 throw. You create two builders, one by slotting your 11-point and one by leaving a third (surplus) checker on your pre-existing point on your 8-point.

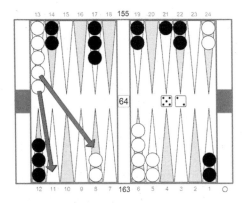

White creates two builders.

ANCHORS

An **anchor** is a point of two or more checkers created in your opponent's home board. There are a number of advantages to creating an anchor.

In the example below, you have thrown a 3+2 and have the chance to make an anchor in Black's home board by moving the checker on your 24-point three spaces to your 21-point, creating an anchor point. You can then play your 2-move safely from your midpoint. With the anchor on your 21-point, you have created a guaranteed place for you to re-enter if you are hit and then manage to throw a 4 in your subsequent turn. Your anchor can give you a number of advantages. Most importantly, you ruin Black's chance of creating a prime of any reasonable length in his home board. Your anchor can also spoil Black's chances of quickly

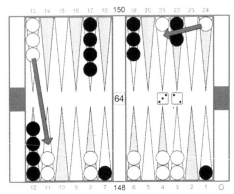

White creates an anchor in Black's home board.

winning a race by disrupting his progress as he tries to get his team home and bear off his checkers. You also give yourself a better chance of freeing your backmarkers from Black's home board later on, and of hitting Black from this position. All of this is achieved with just one anchor, so be on the lookout to create anchors: they can be a great help!

STACKING

Some beginners mistakenly think that you are only allowed to stack a maximum of 5 checkers on one point; this is a myth. Technically there is no limit to how many checkers you can stack on one point, but you'll come to learn that placing too many checkers on any one point is usually a mistake.

On the left, you (White) have stacked seven checkers on one point

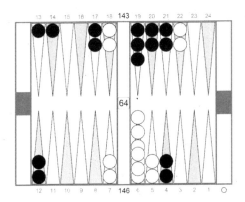

You have stacked seven checkers on your 6-point, which looks clumsy and creates imbalance.

in your home board. Not only does this look clumsy but it also creates an **imbalance** in your game because your last 4 checkers are somewhat marooned at the back. This lack of balance contributes to the fact that Black is the favourite to win this game; you are unlikely to be able to escape easily as you don't have a point in the middle of the board on which to land.

REDUNDANT NUMBERS

Sometimes part or all of your throw cannot legally be taken because you are blocked from doing so. But this is not always as bad as it sounds. For example, on the right, you are easily winning the race but will almost certainly lose if one of your last two checkers is hit before they reach your home board. You've thrown a 6 but *fortunately* you cannot legally move any checker so this 6-move is redundant; you don't have to leave yourself exposed.

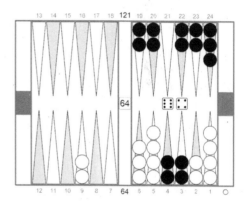

The 6 is redundant as you (White) cannot make a legal move.

JOKERS

Beginners often hear players talking about 'jokers' and have no idea what these players are talking about. A **joker** simply means a very lucky roll that gets a player back into the game when no other combination of dice would have worked (i.e. the unique combination of moves on the dice that are needed for the player to progress with any conceivable chance of winning is rolled). You will often hear players grumbling about their luck turning against them because their opponent has thrown a joker. Jokers are one of the elements that can make backgammon such a thrilling game.

What are you grinning at?

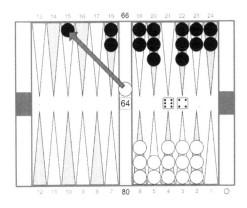

You have thrown a joker with a 6+4 because the 4-move gets you back in the game and the 6-move allows you to hit Black. It is literally the only combination that gives you a chance of winning.

In the position above, Black was clearly winning the game comfortably. There was only one throw that could have resulted in you (White) getting back into the game *and* having a chance of beating Black. This particular throw (6+4) is perfect because it allows you to re-enter with the 4-move and then to hit Black with the 6-move. It completely reverses who is favourite to win the game and it's the only combination of dice that could have done so, which is what makes it a joker.

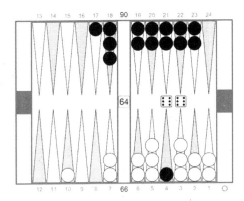

A 6+6 is an anti-joker for White.

ANTI-JOKERS

The opposite of a joker is called an anti-joker. An anti-joker also signifies a complete reversal of fortune, but this time not in your favour. This is a uniquely terrible throw that completely changes your position in the game.

To the left you can see how a 6+6 is a curse in this instance for White (rather than the blessing that it usually is) because you are forced to move 6 places four times. One of these moves will hit Black in your home board, and although this puts his checker on the bar, your next three moves of 6 places will leave two of your checkers exposed, giving him the perfect chance to hit you as he re-enters and stop you in your tracks as you were beginning to bear off. In the diagram below you can see how Black has two opportunities to hit you whilst re-entering the board (by throwing a 4 or a 6). In the example below he throws a 4 and hits your checker on your 4-point. You will only be able to re-enter the game if you throw a 1 in your next roll. Even then you won't be able to move the re-entered checker any further because Black has a 6-point-prime.

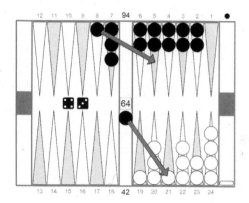

Black throws a 4 and lands White in big trouble.

So, what were your chances of throwing the 6+6 and then what were Black's chances of throwing either a 4 or a 6? It helps to know exactly what your chances are of throwing each combination of dice. We will discuss how to work these out in the chapter called 'Number crunching'.

I've got the (opening) moves like Jagger...

©Corbis Images

6

OPENING
MOVES

*I've gotta get it right the first time
That's the main thing
You get it right the next time,
that's not the same thing*

BILLY JOEL

I remember playing a bold but inexperienced player at a club match in Roehampton. He threw a 5+4 early on in the game and, of all the moves he could make, hit me (White) twice from his 6-point.

This was the very worst thing he could have done. It was a catastrophic blunder

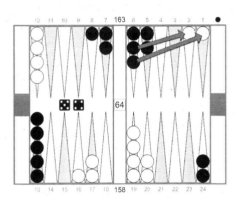

A superbly poor move!

because (according to the XG backgammon software analysis that I entered the moves into later) it reduced my opponent (Black) from being favourite with a 54% chance of winning (had he moved correctly) down to a 31% chance. He had left three of his checkers exposed in his home board while I had two checkers on the bar. The only place I couldn't re-enter on was his 5-point.

To my utter disbelief, I threw an anti-joker: a double 5. After all that, I couldn't move. While the move he made turned out to be extremely lucky for him in this game (primarily caused by my bad luck), I wondered if the experience had actually cost him because it would have left him believing that his move was the right one, which would have set back his progress in learning the game.

OPENING MOVES

Your opening move creates a snowball effect.

How you start the game is crucial; if you make a mistake you could pay for it throughout the game, with compound interest no less. If you start badly, the damage caused to your chances of winning resonates throughout the rest of the game. Many bad moves are made because the player has made a hasty decision and hasn't thought through their options thoroughly. 'Marry in haste… and repent at leisure,' as the saying goes. When it comes to relationships, it is easy to get into one but much harder to get out of one, so you should take care not to make a bad choice. The same goes for backgammon.

Opening moves aren't difficult to get right, yet many players throw away some of their match equity (i.e. give away some of their percentage point chances of winning) at the very start of the game by not bothering to master the best opening moves. There are 21 total possible dice throws, but only 15 are possible opening throws (because you obviously can't start with a double). If you can learn the best opening moves from each of these combinations so well that they become second nature to you, you will be off to a great start in any game. Understanding the best opening moves will help you to think clearly about the game, plus the moves will be much easier to remember if you know why you are making them.

At the start of every game, try to keep in mind what you are trying to achieve. For every move you could make that would help your progress, there is also a move you could make that would most greatly hinder your opponent. As well as seeking to move your checkers around the board quickly, you should also always be looking for opportunities to hinder your opponent's progress, by hitting him or building primes. In a later chapter we will discuss game plans and how you should always have a game plan before you make a decision about any move. Play to your game plan even in your opening move.

We talked earlier about having a good balanced board, so keep this in mind from the outset. Try to **reduce your piles of 5 checkers**, and look for opportunities to **move your backmarkers out**. Conversely, look out for opportunities to stop your opponent from doing this. Even if you can't run your backmarkers all the way to near your midpoint, you can **make an anchor on your opponent's 5-point, 4-point or bar-point**, which will make things difficult for him later.

These are all good priorities to keep in mind for the first few rolls of the game.

So let's look at all 15 possible opening throws, starting with the smallest possible combination and working our way up to the biggest.

2 + 1

Say you throw a 2 and your opponent throws a 1. You might think that this is not the most promising of starts, but at least you get to go first, which is always worth something. Not only does it put you ahead in the race, it can potentially put you ahead in terms of building a strong position. With a 2+1, there are two choices of moves that mean you become a slight favourite at this stage in the game. (Any other move and Black will become a favourite!)

Moving one checker from your 13-point to slot your 11-point begins to unstack your 13-point that has 5 checkers on it. And that loose checker on your 11-point is a builder. It may be useful for building other points and even primes. So now what should you do with the 1-move?

You can either split your backmarkers like this...

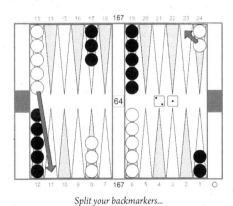

Split your backmarkers...

...or you can make a bolder move by slotting your own 5-point like this...

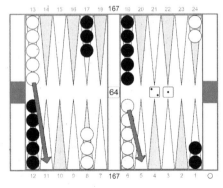

...or slot your 5-point.

These are both strong moves. Moving a backmarker gives you more chances of anchoring further up your opponent's home board (for example by throwing a 4+3 or a 3+2) or of freeing a checker from your opponent's home board early on in the game. But slotting your 5-point is actually a stronger and bolder move.

Note, it's also always a good idea to try to create as many different positive situations with your throw as possible, rather than using up the moves on both dice by making one good move.

The risk of slotting your 5-point is well worth taking. If you are able to convert this blot into a point, you will be in very good shape indeed because you'll have a 2-point-prime in your home board. But if you get hit, it's not the worst thing in the world because it's so early in the game. You are highly likely to be able to re-enter, and even hit back. The early part of the game is the time to make your boldest moves. It's a bit like behaving badly in your twenties – the consequences are usually easier to overcome than they are later in life!

So this is my best recommendation for how to open if you throw a 2+1. Do be aware that Black has the chance of throwing a joker here. If he throws a 6+4 he can hit you twice. And, of course, Murphy's Law states that the first time you try this opening move that is exactly what will happen! But don't let this discourage you, because the chances of Black throwing that joker are still fairly slim, and over the course of many games the odds will even out to your advantage.

3 + 1

In the 1970s, many professionals believed that the best opening throw was a 6+1. In fact, computer analysis now tells us that the best chance of winning the game is if the opening throw is 3+1. It's worth understanding why. A 3+1 is the only opening move with which you can make your own 5-point whilst leaving no other checkers exposed and unsafe. With this move, you have started to box in your opponent's backmarkers with your opening move, and you can start plotting to play with a priming game plan or a hitting game plan (we will come on to describe the different game

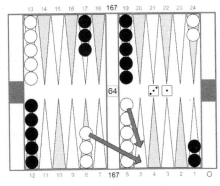

With a 3+1, make your 5-point.

plans in the chapter 'Always have a game plan') If you play this move from a 3+1 opening throw, you instantly become the favourite to win by about 10%. If you play this move from a 3+1 opening throw, you instantly become the favourite to win by about 10%.

The ideal next move, if you throw numbers that allow you to do it, would be to make your bar-point. You would then have a 4-point-prime and be in a very strong early position indeed.

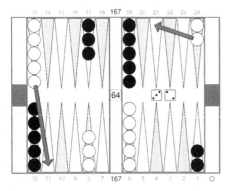

With a 3+2, you can split your backmarkers and slot your 11-point…

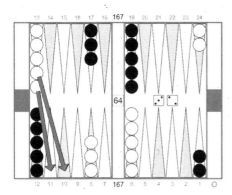

…or move both from the middle to slot two consecutive points.

3 + 2

When you throw a 3+2, you have two choices. Basically, you can split or you can prime. The choice you make depends on how you feel at the time, and the style of play you prefer.

Splitting means separating your two backmarkers with your 3-move by moving one of them along three spaces. With this move, you slot your opponent's 4-point in the home of building an anchor. With your 2-move, you could then take a checker from your midpoint to slot your 11-point in the hope that you throw another 2 with your next roll and you're able to build a point there.

The second choice is to move two checkers from your midpoint to slot both your 11-point and your 10-point (see left) with the expectation of getting the roll that will allow you to build a prime on these consecutive points.

If in doubt, you should play the second choice (slotting your 11-point and 10-point with a view to priming), as it is the more aggressive move and we are still so early on in the game that it's worth taking the risk.

4 + 1

Your best opening move with a throw of 4+1 depends largely on who your opponent is. Computer analysis won't necessarily help you here because the computer will always assume you are playing the world champion. If you are playing a weaker opponent, you can slot both your 9-point and your 5-point like this...

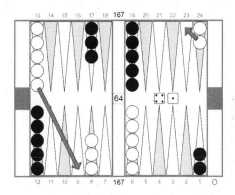

*The best move with a 4+1 if you're
playing against a chump...*

Even though it's risky leaving two blots on your side of the board, if your risk pays off you could build a winning lead. Even if it doesn't, because you are playing against a weak player you may well have chances of recovering the game later.

If you are playing against a strong player, you might not want to leave two blots on your side of the board for your opponent's backmarkers to hit; it's just too much of a risk because if both your blots get hit by a strong opponent, you're in real trouble. If you're playing against a champ, it's better just to slot your 9-point and then move a backmarker with your 1-move, where it doesn't matter much if you are hit, and this also gives you more options for moving your backmarkers out. Now you are leaving a couple of blots where it's less serious if they're hit.

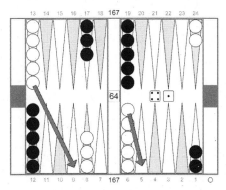

...and if you're playing against a champ.

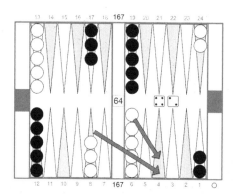

With a 4+2 throw, make your 4-point.

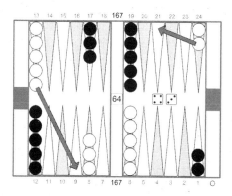

With a 4+3, either split the backmarkers…

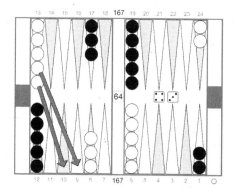

…or move two from the middle.

4 + 2

This move is very straightforward. The best move is to make your 4-point. No other option comes close. It's not quite as good as that killer 3+1 opener, but it's still pretty good.

4 + 3

This is similar to the 3+2: you can split your backmarkers and move one checker from your midpoint to slot your 9-point, or you can move both checkers from the midpoint.

With a throw of 4+3, splitting your backmarkers often has the edge because you can leave a blot in your opponent's home board on his 4-point or 5-point in the hope that you'll be able to make an anchor on it soon. While you might be tempted to slot his 5-point with your 4-move instead of slotting his 4-point with your 3-move (partly because you know it will distract him to see you sitting there), the better use of your 4-move is to move a checker from your midpoint to your 9-point (as shown below) because it gives you the opportunity to make a 2-point-prime if you get a 4 in your next throw.

As with the 3+2, there is a more aggressive move (and therefore my favourite!) You can move two checkers from your midpoint onto your

9-point and 10-point. If the priming opportunities you have created pan out, you have a strong chance of winning, and might even win a double game (as we will see in the chapter on doubling). This is my top pick.

5 + 3

Very similar to the 3+1 and the 4+2, this is another straightforward, strong opening move: you make your 3-point safely.

Although this isn't as exciting as making your 5-point (with the 3+1) or your 4-point (with the 4+2), it's still a good home-board point and you'll only need to make another point before you'll be in the strong position of having three home-board points.

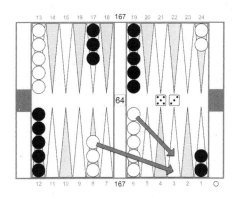

With a throw of 5+3, make your 3-point.

It's interesting to note that back in the 1970s and early 1980s, before the computer analysis of backgammon, virtually all the experts agreed that the best opening play with a 5+3 was to bring a couple of checkers down from point 13, the midpoint. Everyone did it because the best players and teachers said it was the right thing to do. And there are still some old-timers who continue to make what is often a wrong move. Right off the bat they are giving away about 9% equity. In other words, their chances decrease by 9% by making this move instead of building their 3-point. Let's hope they don't buy this book before you meet them in a tournament!

5 + 4

There's not much choice about what to do with your 5-move; you move a checker from your midpoint onto your 8-point, leaving you an extra builder.

Now you are left with a couple of

With a 5+4, move a builder onto your 8-point and slot your opponent's 5-point.

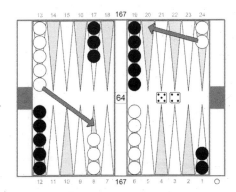

choices for the 4-move. You could slot Black's 5-point or you could slot your 9-point. It's generally better to slot your opponent's 5-point to give you a chance of making an anchor, so that's the one I recommend.

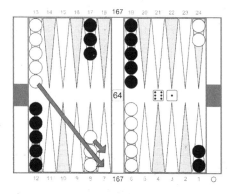

6 + 1

This is a no-brainer. You make your bar-point. With this move you have built a 3-point-prime on your opening move. This is a *great* opening move.

With a 6+1, make your bar-point.

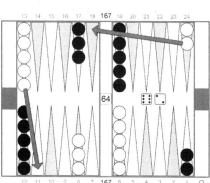

With a 6+2, move one from the back and one from the middle.

6 + 2

With a 6+2 opening throw, you have a couple of choices. You could combine the values and run a backmarker eight spaces. However, as I've mentioned before, it's always best to start two initiatives, using both your dice numbers rather than combining them. The best option with a 6+2 throw is to run one of your backmarker 6 pips with your 6-move and then slot your 11-point with your 2-move.

6 + 3

This is very similar to 6+2. You move one of your backmarkers forward with your 6-move and then slot your 10-point (as opposed to your 11-point with the 6+2).

With a 6+3 throw, you take one from the back and one from the middle.

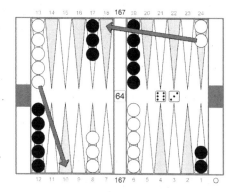

6 + 4

With a throw of 6+4, the obvious move is to follow the pattern with the 3+1, 4+2 and 5+3 and make your 2-point. To any beginner, this would seem a natural and obvious move.

However, checkers on your 2-point can't really play much of an active part for the rest of the game. Many more experienced players would move a backmarker (to slot your opponent's bar-point) and move a midmarker to slot your 9-point as this gives you more potential to build a more effective prime. This choice is what I would always recommend if you have a 6+4 to start.

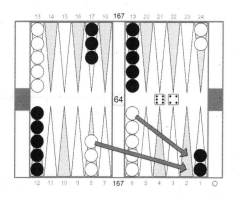

With a 6+4, either make your 2-point...

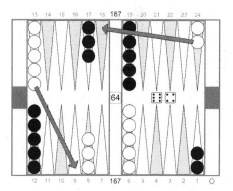

...or free a backmarker and slot your 9-point.

6 + 5

So that just leaves us with the highest starting throw. The best move with a 6+5 is (for once) to combine the dice and move a backmarker all the way to your midpoint. In one fell swoop you only have one backmarker and a big lead. There's no need to think about any other choices. This move is so well known, it has been given a name: *Lover's Leap* (although I'm not sure why, when you are splitting *apart* your two backmarkers!)

So those are your best opening moves. You should memorize your

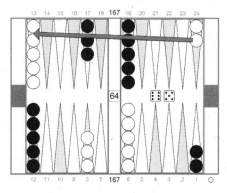

6+5; good old Lover's Leap!

favourite opening moves so that you have one less thing to think about at the beginning of each game. A strong opening move will give you a solid foundation for the rest of the game. Even if you don't go first, it helps to know these moves so you know how to reply to them. This is another crucial part of the game, and one we will examine in the next chapter.

The great Mickey Rooney – loved backgammon and loved
replying to opening moves (just ask his eight wives!)

Image Chicagopoint.com

7

THE EARLY
GAME

First look for a great play,
and then find a better one.

PHIL SIMBORG

When I was a teenager I lived in London with my mother and her boyfriend Ken Havard. Ken was an avid backgammon player and, to me, seemed to play wonderfully well in spite of the huge quantities of Valpolicella he consumed. I watched him eagerly, even though it was often hard to see the board through the clouds of smoke produced by the Rothmans King Size cigarettes he chain-smoked. Sometimes I found myself in the hot seat opposite him and we always played for money, even if the stakes were modest.

Ken would try to seize the advantage early on, trying to put me off by commentating while I was trying to think. If I threw a double, he would cackle, 'Doubles, doubles...', inferring that I was playing with more than my fair share of luck.

Ken knew all the opening moves and replies by heart. This is no mean feat. In the first two throws there are 315 possible different dice combinations: 15 possible first throws (remember, no doubles in the first throw) and 21 potential throws in reply, so there is a huge number of choices, even at this early stage.

I never had a chance!

REPLYING TO THE OPENING MOVE

Unlike Ken, I'm not going to suggest you try to memorise all the possible reply moves on top of all the opening moves; it's more important to understand why you would want to make a particular move.

As with the opening move, it's important to focus on moving your backmarkers, unstacking your checkers, starting to make important points (your 4-point, 5-point and bar-point, and those of your opponent) and planning primes. And, of course, in your reply to the opening move you may be the first player to get a chance to hit, if your opponent has left any blots after his opening move.

You should continue to prioritize these strategies beyond the opening two moves and as the game continues. In fact, good questions to ask yourself every turn in the early stages of the game (and indeed beyond) are: **Can I hit?**, **Can I make a point?** and **Can I play strategically?** in that order. We will discuss these strategies in more detail when we come to talk about game plans.

Let's look at those doubles first.

1 + 1

This is a peach of a throw to get in reply to an opening move. Usually you can make a great 3-point-prime by making your 5-point and your bar-point, as shown in the example on the right.

The only time you should think twice about this move is if your opponent has split his backmarkers in his opening move. This would make him more likely to hit the blot you've left on your 8-point. In this scenario, still make your 5-point with two of your 1-moves but with the other two 1-moves split up your backmarkers (as shown on the right). It's still a good move because you've made your 'golden' 5-point and have split your backmarkers; you've achieved two key objectives with one throw and protected yourself against getting hit on your 8-point.

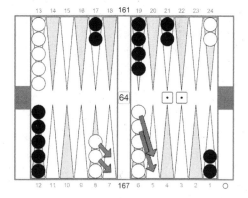

With a 1+1, build a 3-point-prime.

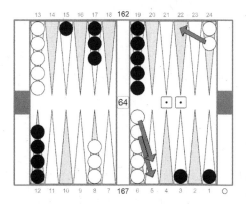

With a 1+1, if your opponent has split his markers, make your 5-point and split your backmarkers.

2 + 2

This is another good throw. Always make your 4-point and (nearly always) move two of your midmarkers, like this...

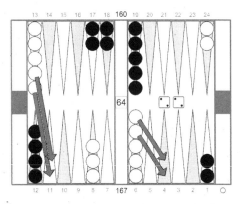

With a 2+2, make your 4-point and move two midmarkers.

If your opponent has already made his 4-point or 5-point, however, you should move your backmarkers along instead of moving your midmarkers, as you need to avoid getting boxed in. So still make your 4-point, but move your backmarkers along two spaces...

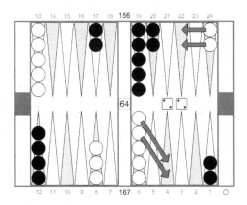

With a 2+2, if your opponent has made his 4-point or 5-point,
you should still make your 4-point but then move your backmarkers along
two spaces instead of your midmarkers.

3 + 3

A 3+3 is another lovely roll. Here's a great chance to make a second and third inner-board-point very early on.

Again, if your opponent has already started to hem you in by making his bar-point and/or 5-point, then it's best to start getting those backmarkers outta Dodge City. If this is the case, move your backmarkers and you could also move your midmarkers to keep your board very well balanced.

This move is not set in stone. For instance, if you have the chance to hit you should probably do that as a priority, so stay flexible. As ever, scan the board for the best opportunity.

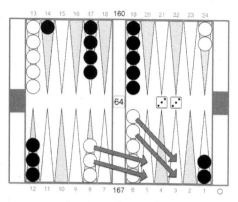

A 3+3 is a great opportunity to make your 5-point and 3-point.

4 + 4

It's almost impossible to do a bad reply with a throw of 4+4 as you have so many good choices.

A strong option is to make your opponent's 5-point and move two checkers from your midpoint (as shown on the right).

If you can't do this because your opponent has already made his 5-point, you could move straight

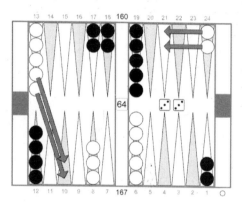

If your opponent is making a strong prime, start mobilising the troops!

With a 4+4, make your opponent's 5-point and your own 8-point.

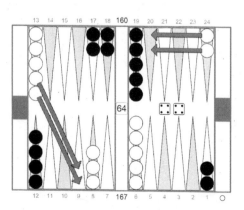

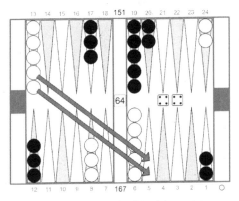

*If your opponent has already made his 5-point,
use a 4+4 to move straight from your midpoint to
make your own 5-point.*

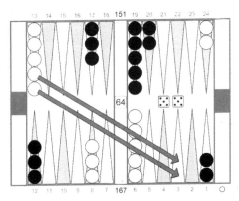

*With a 5+5 it's best to move straight from
your midpoint to make your 3-point.*

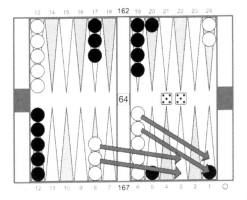

from your midpoint to make your own 5-point. This is also a very strong move.

Once again, look for alternatives (e.g. opportunities to hit) and stay flexible.

5 + 5

Although this looks like a good throw because it's a high number, it's actually the worst double to get early on. You can't move the back-markers, and moving the midmarkers doesn't help you build a prime. Usually it's best to move the midmarkers to make your 3-point.

If your opponent has split his backmarkers with his opening move, the 5+5 might not be such a bad throw. You can move two checkers from your 6-point to hit his and make your 1-point, and then move two checkers from your 8-point to make your 3-point, leaving you with three home points and slashing your opponent's odds of throwing a number that allows him to re-enter the board. This hitting approach is called 'blitzing', as it will likely seriously hold up your opponent because he can't continue until he can re-enter the board. This could lead to a very quick death for your opponent.

*If your opponent has split his backmarkers,
you can blitz him with a 5+5.*

6 + 6

As long as your opponent didn't start with a 6-1 and make his bar-point, a 6+6 can be one of the best rolls you can throw. You get to make both your bar-point and your opponent's bar-point, giving you a huge leap in the race.

If you are blocked from doing this because your opponent has already made his bar-point, you'll have to improvise. Your next best option is to make your bar-point (in preparation for building a 3-point-prime) and make your 2-point to hem in your opponent's backmarkers, as shown on the right.

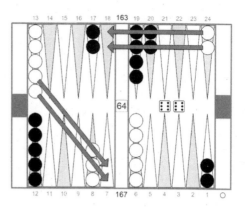

If possible, with a 6+6 you should make your opponent's bar-point and your own bar-point.

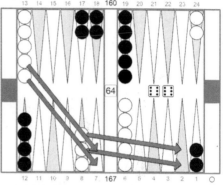

If blocked from making your opponent's bar-point, make your bar-point and your 2-point.

NON-DOUBLES

There are 15 other potential throws we can get if we don't throw a double. We have already looked at all of these moves as we would play them as opening moves, but do our choices change significantly when we throw them in reply to our opponent's opener? In many cases, we would make exactly the same choices we would have made if we had thrown the dice combination as an opening move. However, in some cases we need to make different choices to counter our opponent's opening.

Here are some examples...

PLAYING A 3+1 IF...

a) Black already occupies your 5-point...
When you throw a 3+1, your classic best opening move in reply opponent to your opponent's opening is to make a point on your 5-point. However, there are a couple of opening

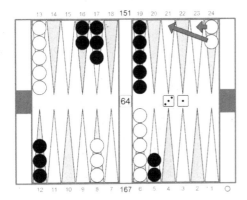

moves by your opponents that should give you pause. For example, what should you do if Black has already made your 5-point? In this scenario, the best choice is to break up your backmarkers. This is a safer choice than moving your midmarkers and leaving blots exposed closer to home.

b) Black has slotted his 5-point...
If Black has slotted his 5-point, it's actually better to hit him than to make your own 5-point. It's especially damaging to him because you are hitting him in his home board and this checker will have to start right back at the beginning. In general, if ever in doubt... hit!

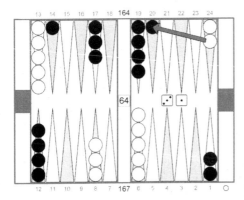

The best use of your 3+1 if Black has slotted his 5-point is to hit him with one of your backmarkers.

PLAYING A 6+5 IF...

Black has slotted your bar-point
The classic opening move with a 6+5 is Lover's Leap. However, if your opponent has slotted your bar-point you might think twice before making that famous move. In the scenario shown on the left, your best option is to hit him twice. There is a good chance he won't get both checkers in on his next throw

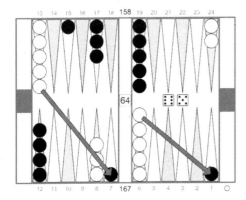

If your opponent has slotted your bar-point, go for the double hit with a 6+5.

and may have to skip one or more turns. This will give you the opportunity to build a strong advantage. It's risky, but a double hit is usually the best way to go.

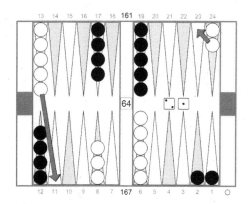

If you throw a 2+1 after Black breaks up his backmarkers, mirror his actions.

PLAYING A 2+1 IF...

a) Your opponent has split his backmarkers...

If your opponent has split his backmarkers and you throw a good old 2+1, it no longer makes sense to slot your 5-point and move from your midpoint because you would be too vulnerable. In this scenario it's better to split your backmarkers, as shown above.

b) Black has made a second point on his home board...

If Black has made a second point on his home board, it again makes sense to break up your backmarkers with your 1-move. In the scenario shown below you can see how it's best to start mobilising your backmarkers. Splitting them up gives you more chances of escaping and of hitting your opponent. With your 2-move, begin to unstack your midmarkers and slot your 11-point.

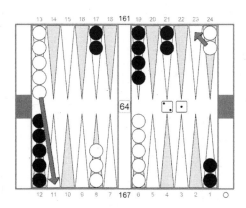

With a 2+1, if Black has made a second point in his home board, it's best to break up your backmarkers and unstack your midmarkers.

Looking more closely at this scenario, notice how Black now has only two checkers on his 8-point. That's also the signal to split up your backmarkers, because Black is limited as to how he can use those checkers on his next roll. If he throws a 3+1, a 6+1 or a 5+3 (ordinarily all good throws) he's less likely to split up his checkers on his 8-point to hit you because he would become too vulnerable to being hit himself. This example shows you how you should always think ahead to what might happen with your opponent's next roll. It's always a smart strategy to think ahead before you make a decision about how to move.

Now that you have an understanding of how to play *your* opening move, and how to play a *reply* to your opponent's opening move, you are already streets ahead of the player who sleepwalks through the start of the game. Hopefully, you will also already be much calmer and more composed than your average opponent in these early stages of the game.

Photo Corbis Images

*The legendary James Hunt, adrenaline junkie,
in one of numerous photos of him playing backgammon.*

8

THE MIDDLE GAME

Now this is not the end.
It is not even the beginning of the end.
But it is, perhaps, the end of the beginning.

WINSTON CHURCHILL

I
n the quarter final of a tournament at Brooks's Club in London, I was offered an early double. My opponent, Milo, was young and confident. He was polite but boarding on aloof. He wore a silk waistcoat, and was smiling and making strange little sounds through his hipster beard. We both needed our props: he was sucking on a plastic cigarette and ordered a 'mocktail'. I asked for a decaf coffee. E-cig, mocktail, decaf... the only genuine article on the table was the board!

Playing a match to 5 points is either brutally or blissfully short depending on whether or not you're winning. We were at 1-1. In the next game, Milo offered me a double in a game. I felt he had only a slight advantage, so I was seriously considering it. As I pondered the offer, he stared at me and continued his little grunting noises, increasingly reminding me of a hamster. In the end, I accepted the double but as soon as I did I regretted it, not least because I realised too late that if he won a gammon (i.e. double the double... 4 points from this one game), we would be at 5-1. He would have won the match and I'd be out of the tournament. The feeling that he knew something I didn't waved across me.

Pretty soon, I could see that my timing was better than his and I doubled him back. Now the match was mine for the taking because a win was worth four points to me. It felt invigorating, like going 'all in' in poker. As pleased as he seemed, I couldn't help feeling he had got this wrong. I really thought I was in with a chance, but I wasn't completely sure. My spirits rose as I started to take an even greater advantage, and soon I was in a very strong position. Finally we were in a position where the game was almost certainly mine. I had most of my checkers in the home board and had made 5 of my 6 home-board points. I had hit him with my last throw so he was dancing on the bar (as shown in the diagram below). There was only one way he had a chance of getting back into the game and that was by throwing a 5, hitting me back and putting me on the bar and then racing me home. As long as he didn't throw that 5, I was almost certain to win. I held my breath as he threw the dice and...

... he got the 5! It seemed only a few seconds later that he was shaking my hand and I was wishing him good luck and goodnight before heading home!

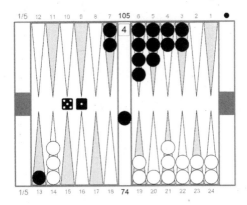

Milo needs a 5... and gets it!

It's important to spot when you are have arrived in the middle of things. As Michael Caine once said, 'People call me middle-aged and I'm 60. Well I don't know that many 120-year-olds, do you?'

There comes a point in some games where, early on, it can become a straight race with nobody being hit and nobody being blocked. If this happened all the time, backgammon would be as dull as a power cut on a rainy day. Happily, it is a rare event. Usually someone gets hit, someone gets blocked, someone's backmarkers are trapped and so on. When some of this has started to happen and each player has had 4 or 5 moves, then you know that you've reached **the middle game**.

GAME PLANS

One of the golden rules in backgammon is... **always have a game plan.** You should have a game plan in your head before you make a decision about every single move. However, it's never more important to have a game plan than in the middle game. Every game is different and you need to play a lot of games so that you can practice what to do when you come across different situations. Generally, your game plan should be one of three specific strategies: run, hit or prime.

If you have the upper hand in the middle game, it's usually quite easy to decide which of the three game plans is best. But when you are behind in the game, it's often hard to see which strategy could help you win. In this situation, you need to watch your opponent closely to work out which game plan he is following and then use a counter-tactic to foil him.

The important middle-game tactics include keeping a **balanced board**, moving any **stragglers at the back** around the board, hampering your opponent's progress by **hitting** and **priming**, **slotting** where you can and **creating anchors**. And you must always **stay flexible**, as you usually won't get the dice you want.

In the middle game, continually ask yourself questions about how the game stands. How strong is your opponent's home board? How many points has he made? Does he have any blots? Does he have checkers stuck in your home board? Do you have any stuck in his? Always consider your own position, too. If you're doing better than him, you can afford to be more aggressive.

SPLITTING BACKMARKERS

If you have yet to move your backmarkers and you're approaching the middle game, it's time to look for opportunities to get them moving, which will usually mean splitting them.

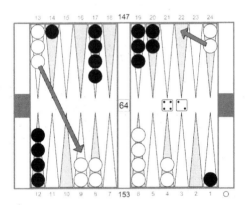

With a 4+2 in this scenario, splitting your backmarkers and moving one from the midpoint is your best option.

In the example shown above, you have already thrown a 4+2 and made your 4-point, so when you throw a 4+2 for a second time, the best option is to split the backmarkers. This gives you multiple chances of reuniting the two checkers, or of running with one of them. If you don't do this, Black could close in on you, especially as he has already freed one backmarker with a lover's leap move. You will be in a pickle if you don't act soon. In any case, in this situation there's not a lot else you can productively do with your throw.

BUILDING PRIMES THROUGH SLOTTING

Building primes can be a messy business. In the example below, you have a number of options with your throw of 5+4. You can make another home-board point on your 2-point, or you can slot your opponent's 5-point and slot your own 8-point from your midpoint. But what kind of game are you playing? Clearly you are losing in the race, so you don't want to run. You have a modest home board and no clear opportunities to hit, so hitting is not an available plan. You already have a 3-point-prime made; so continuing to build your prime looks like your best game plan.

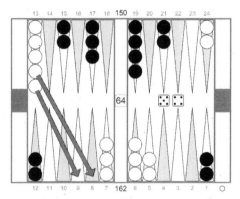

*With a 5+4 your best move is to slot both your 8-point
and 9-point, leaving two builders on them.*

This looks risky, but it's still fairly early on in the game and your opponent's home board is not strong yet; it makes sense for you to take some risks. You could make your 2-point, but not only is that disconnected from your existing strong prime, it also takes those two checkers out of the running for making more valuable points on your 3-point and 4-point. Your best bet is to move two checkers from your midpoint to slot your 8 and 9 points, creating two **builders** with the hope that you will be able to turn them into points with your next move, strengthening your prime. It looks risky but Black would need to throw a 7 or 8 to hit you – he cannot hit you with one dice – so his chances of scuppering your game plan are reduced. The opportunities to prime from this position, assuming you are not hit, are so good it's worth the risk. As long as those builders don't get hit, there are many throws that will enable you to make your 8-point or 9-point. Another 4+5 would even allow you to make both. You also have an opportunity to make your 4-point if you throw a 3+2, so you are well on your way to making a 6-point-prime, the ultimate prime. If this priming game plan pays off, Black is toast.

Let's look at another example.

In the scenario shown on the right, you are much more vulnerable because your backmarkers are split. Rather than slotting both your 9-point and 10-point here, you should definitely take the opportunity to make your opponent's 4-point. You can still leave a valuable builder by using one of your midmarkers to slot your 9-point, which will hopefully be the start of a strong prime. You should always be looking for ways to create a prime in and around your home board.

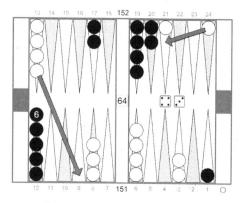

With a 4+3 in this scenario, make your opponent's 4-point and slot your 9-point with your midmarker.

BLITZING

Blitzing is a thrilling strategy, one that really makes the game exciting. I always love a good blitz and I am sure you will too! It is a battle of nerves. While your opponent is desperately trying to get a foothold in your home board, you **blitz** him, hitting him again and again regardless of your own exposure. There is no faster way to win a game. Furthermore, you give yourself a

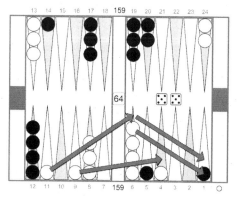

5+5 gives you many choices, but to hit and make two extra home-board points is best.

strong chance of winning by a large margin and therefore gammoning your opponent, earning you double points in the process.

In the example shown above, you have many choices of how to play your 5+5. The most compelling is to create two more points in your home board, while hitting your opponent and giving you further opportunities to hit.

Often both sides can be blitzing each other at the same time, which is even more fun.

The position below is slightly different, but you are still able to hit black and make two more home-board points. You do end up with one checker exposed on the 1-point in your home board but it's worth it for the thrill of the blitz. And with a bit of luck you'll soon be able to cover the exposed blot.

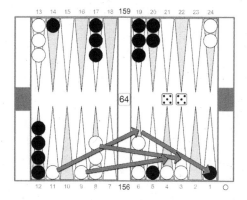

With your 5+5 in this scenario, you can hit and make three more home-board points.

DUPLICATION AND DIVERSIFICATION

Don't be put off by these words that sound like you'd only use them if you were doing a PhD in Economics! They simply describe a great way to improve your odds at a point when your opponent will likely have multiple ways to hurt you in his next move. You need to play in a way that limits his chances to do too much damage.

Duplication means duplicating your opponent's need to throw a specific number in order to do maximum damage – i.e. decreasing his chances of really hurting you.

In the example below, the race is close unless you are hit. You have thrown a 6+2 and you are forced to move your 6-move from Black's home board; there is no other option with the 6-move. So the question now is what to do with the 2-move. In this scenario, you should continue to move the same checker a further two spaces so that it lands on your 11-point because now Black will need a 3 to hit either of your checkers, i.e. he would need a double 3 to hit both. If you do anything else with your 2-move (e.g. move one of the checkers in your home board or move your other backmarker 2 spaces), you still have two exposed checkers but Black needs *different numbers* to hit you,

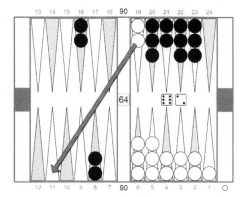

With a 6+2 you can duplicate Black's need to throw a 3.

which greatly *increases* his chances of hitting one or both of your blots. The move shown below **duplicates** Black's need to throw a 3 to hit you, i.e. he can only do the maximum damage (of hitting you twice) if he throws a 3+3. This is quite a nifty little tactic!

Diversification means giving yourself as many chances as possible of achieving something.

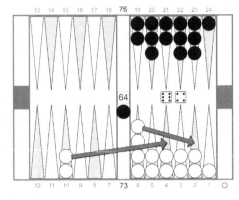

A 6+4 allows you to diversify your options, giving you the best chance to cover your blot next time.

In the game on the left, you have thrown a 6+4. While you cannot cover your blot without leaving another checker exposed, you can give yourself as many shots as possible to do so with your next turn. In this case, instead of moving both your checkers into the home board (one of which would land on your 6-point that already holds spare checkers), if you move a checker from your 6-point to your 2-point, creating a builder there, you have a much larger number of throws that could allow you to cover the blot without exposing another one next time.

IT AIN'T OVER 'TIL IT'S OVER

If all of your opponent's checkers have escaped and you are still moving yours around the board, you might think there is no point in building more home-board points and strengthening a prime. However, you might still want to hit your opponent and then you need that strong home board. So keep working on building that prime!

I often see players who are losing a race focus on moving their checkers around the board as quickly as possible. A better game plan when you are in this situation is to hit, even if you can't immediately see where that opportunity to hit is going to come from. So you must keep preparing. Pretend that you have your opponent trapped and build that prime anyway. When he sees your game plan is to keep building rather than racing, your opponent will likely slow down and play more cautiously. This, in turn, will give you a greater chance of winning if and when you *do* get to hit your opponent, which actually happens more often than you would think!

On the right you have thrown 5+4, so one option one option would be to race your backmarker out, but that would be a mistake because it engages you in a race *you are already losing*. Building your home board is the better strategy. If you get the opportunity to hit your opponent later (and you are leaving your backmarker in place for exactly that possibility), a strong home board will hamper your opponent's chances of re-entering the

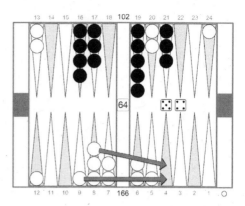

Keep building that prime even though he's gone...
you will need it when you get the chance to hit him later!

board and increase your chances of winning. If you leave a weak and vulnerable home board, even if you get to hit your opponent, they could do equal damage by hitting you back in your home board.

PICK AND PASS

Pick and pass refers to hitting your opponent with one of your moves, and then moving to safety with the other. In the example below, you could make Black's 5-point with that single backmarker. But a much better move is to hit Black's checker on your 5-point with

your 3-move and then bounce your checker to safety with the 4-move, making your 1-point (sometimes called the '**ace-point**'). You've achieved two things here – hitting and creating a home-board point – without taking much risk. Plus, with Black having to waste at least one of his moves by having to re-enter on his next throw, you will probably be in with a strong chance of moving your backmarkers out with your next move.

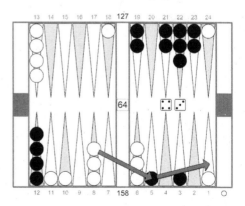

With your 4+3, land on Black then bounce safely
onto your own checker to make your 1-point.

BLOCK A PAIR AND ATTACK A BLOT

If your opponent still has both his backmarkers (i.e. a **pair**) in your home board, it is well worth continuing to build points and primes to block him. This will make it increasingly difficult for him to move them out. If he only has one backmarker left in your home board (i.e. a **blot**), it is less worthwhile blocking him because he could get away with one good throw, so you might as well look for opportunities to hit him (as long as you have a strong home board).

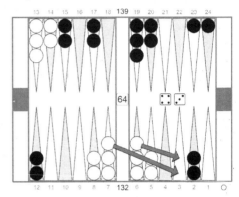

Blocking a pair. With this 4+3 make your 3-point, but only if you Black has both backmarkers in your home board.

You can use your throw of 4+3 on the right to build your 3-point against Black's pair is a must. In any case, you don't have an alternative play that is particularly useful. Remember, every play you make is only good or bad in comparison to the alternatives. The golden rule is: **whenever you see a play you think is good, see if there is another play that is better before you commit.**

Looking at a similar situation but one where Black only has one backmarker, it becomes less important to block him. Unless you have a safe way of hitting him, it is more important to run, like this...

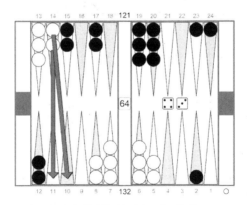

Against a blot, blocking is less of a priority.

WHEN TO BREAK UP
AN ANCHOR

It is always useful to have an anchor in your opponent's board; the question becomes when to run. In the position on the right, you have thrown a 5+4. You could run one checker from the back with this, but a better move is to take two checkers from the middle and make your 9-point, which gives you another 2-point-prime.

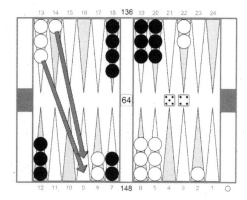

In this scenario, keep hold of that anchor in your opponent's home board.

In this next exaxmple, you have already broken up your anchor and have been left with one checker at the back. It would make much more sense to run because you are more vulnerable. And, of course, you can't cause as much trouble as you can with two checkers forming an anchor in your opponent's home board.

Phil Simborg has a checklist to help decide when to break an anchor. Ask yourself:

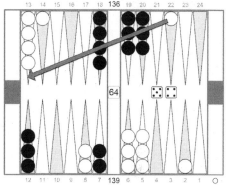

Time to get out of Dodge.

1. Who is up in the race?
2. What is my best game plan?
3. Who has the stronger inner board?
4. If I run with one checker, how likely is it that the remaining checker will be approached or attacked?
5. Do I have a better alternative on the other side of the board?

The answers to these questions will help you to decide whether it's a good time to break the anchor.

WATCH YOUR OPPONENT'S HOME BOARD
IN THE MIDDLE GAME

In the position shown below, you have recently escaped clean out of Black's home board. You have made your opponent's bar-point and you are now on a roll, while Black still has two backmarkers stuck in your home board.

Who do you think is favourite to win the game at this stage?

Well, it may surprise you to hear that Black is actually the favourite to win. The odds are that you will get hit before the end of the game. If this happens, Black has a very strong home board and will be likely block you from re-entering. As a result of either not getting the right throws or a lack of foresight, you have not diversified your checkers enough and will probably soon find yourself in a spot of hot water. You would have to be very lucky to bring

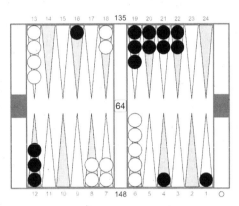

Even though you have escaped from Black's home board while he still has checkers in yours... Black is favourite to win because of his lead in the pip count, his strong home board and your unbalanced board.

all of your checkers home without giving Black several opportunities to hit you.

If you had taken a few more chances earlier, like slotting and bringing builders down from the midpoint, before Black's board was so well established, you might not have got into this predicament.

In general, in the middle game you should aim to keep all your checkers in play. As far as possible you should avoid moving them so far along that they become redundant. If you have several stacked on the last point in your home board (your 1-point), you have less checkers in your army. You need your checkers in the game, ready to build defences and attack your opponent. Checkers are no use to you in the final places of your home board too early on in the game.

Fred Astaire achieves compatability with two stripes of varying spacing.

J Epstein, "The Astaire Way to Paradise," The Hudson Review.

Fred Astaire looks very relaxed considering the cube is on 32.

9

THE ENDGAME

*Some winners tend to play rapidly,
but most play a little more slowly than average.
Even the fast players among them don't rush things,
and if an unusually difficult play comes up,
they will take the time they need.*

WALTER TRICE, 2004

I was once playing a match at a party at Home House club in Marylebone, in London. My opponent, Cedric, was chatty and charming and seemed much more confident than me. I tried not to let my nerves show.

I won the first game easily in which after establishing a lead I offered him a double. He declined, forfeiting the game, so it was 1-0 to me. In the next game, I accepted a double offered by him but went on to lose. So I went 1-2 down. The same thing happened again, rather quickly. So now I was 1-4 down in a game to 5. Disaster! I could feel my heart start to beat faster and experienced that panicky, catastrophic, crushing feeling, as if someone had just said, ominously, 'The headmaster wants to see you in his study.'

Cedric started murdering me in the next game. I noticed a crowd had gathered to watch the match. Eventually I counted 10 people standing around us, watching and whispering. I knew two people at this party but they were nowhere to be seen. I had to play what is known as a **back game** (a strategy that gives you a chance of winning when you are losing!) It was my only chance because he was so far ahead of me on pips. I was rapidly losing the race. I managed to get myself hit several times and was thus able to build a 2-point-prime deep in his home board.

I could see that I was now very likely to get a shot at him, but I don't think many people watching realized this, to whom it seemed I was being thrashed. In actual fact, at this stage in the game I was favourite to win the game because I would have many opportunities to hit my opponent. Finally, he left a checker exposed and

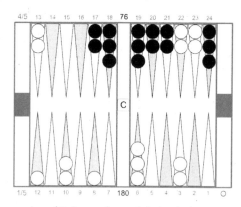

I am white. I am 1-4 down and playing a back game.

I just needed a 5. My luck came in. I rolled the dice and... bingo! Out popped the 5! My luck carried me through and I ended up winning. So now I was 2-4 down. My luck continued into the next game and I won a double game, which evened up the score to 4-4.

Finally it all rested on one final game. It was cut and thrust with a lot of hitting, but eventually I saw my chance to run home and I took it. I was ahead by about 12 pips.

Then Cedric threw a 6+6 followed by a 4+4, which destroyed my lead. He won.

Despite the fact that I'd been beaten I was still pleased with my performance. I'd kept it together and played the best I could. I'd played a thrilling match against an excellent opponent. I had enjoyed that last game so much – much more than the earlier ones – that I really didn't mind losing. It was 2.30 a.m. by then and the adrenaline was surging through my veins. I was fairly sure that sleep was off the table for that night!

ALWAYS HAVE A GAME PLAN

As you reach the later stages of each game, it's more important than ever to remember the golden rule: **always have a game plan**.

So let's look at some examples showing games in their later stages and discuss what your game plan should be in each scenario. Remember the basic game plans are: **hitting**, **priming** and **running**.

In the example below, you are being thrashed in the race (look at the difference in pip counts). But then you throw a 6+6. There is no point in continuing to extend your prime because Black has freed his backmarkers and you are losing in the race so running is not an option. So what game plan does that leave you with? The answer here is **hitting**. Even though, at the moment you don't have a potential hit in sight, you should be preparing for it. And in preparation you need to build you home board in order to reduce Black's chances of

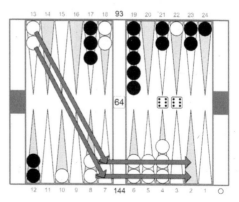

With the 6+6, keep building your home board, preparing for that hit you hope to get later.

re-entering when, hopefully, you do get the chance to hit him. You also need to keep those backmarkers in place ready to hit as soon as the opportunity arises.

Don't give in to the temptation to move your backmarkers out with your big throw. Create another point in your home board and, with each successive throw keep building in your home board and waiting for the opportunity to hit; it's your only chance to catch up with Black.

PIP COUNT

You must always stay aware of the pip count. This is especially important in these later stages of the game. When you are playing a computer, or online, the computer will always calculate the pips for you. So you need to make sure you can do it in your head when you're playing on a real board. Get used to counting the pips quickly as you don't want to hold up play too much!

HOLDING GAMES

A holding game is one in which you hold onto an anchor in your opponent's home board. It can be very useful to keep your anchor as it could seriously scupper your opponent's efforts to run home. However, at some point you will have to release it and run yourself. Also, when you hold a high point in your opponent's board, such as his 4-point or 5-point, or even his bar-point, he can never build an effective prime to block you. The example below shows you in a holding game. You have an anchor on your opponent's 5-point.

You are holding your anchor with a view to getting the opportunity to hit your opponent so, while you are waiting, you *must* build a strong home board. With your

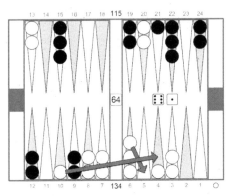

Build your home board and cross your fingers that you will get a shot.

throw of 6+1 in the scenario shown above, you could run a backmarker safely to the midpoint. However, running is the last thing you want to do when you are already behind in the race (look at the pip count). The better play is to build your home board and hope for the hit that will help you catch up. (If you had a similar board but were significantly ahead in the race, however, you might as well run.)

When you are in a holding game you must always consider the trade-off between escaping and being gammoned. If your opponent has a point in your home board, the deeper it is the greater the threat that he will hit you as you bear off. You are similarly at risk when your opponent is on the bar because any exposed checker you leave while bearing off is a potential hit for him. In these cases, you need to keep a tidy home board and avoid leaving exposed checkers.

Conversely, if it's you holding an anchor deep in your opponent's home board, ensure you have built a formidable fortress in your home board before you relinquish your anchor in order to make that hit.

There does come a time in a holding game where, if you hang around any longer you are at risk of losing a gammon and therefore going down by double the points that the game is worth at that stage. This is the time to stack your checkers as high as you like; don't waste a single pip in getting your checkers into your home board. But conversely, do everything in your power to stop your opponent from releasing his anchor (by not giving him opportunities to hit you) so that you have a chance of winning a gammon yourself. Be bold: a gammon is very valuable, especially if a double has already been offered, which makes it worth 4 points!

ACE-POINT GAMES

John Lennon said, 'Life is what happens while you're making plans,' and never is this more true than when you are winning but your opponent still has two checkers in place on your 1-point. This is called an **ace-point game** and it can seriously mess up your plans!

Looking at it from your point of view, holding your opponent's 1-point (ace-point) is not as strong as having a back game with two points held in your opponent's home board, or even holding one point but higher up his board (such as his 2-point or 3-point), but you do still have a very good chance of hitting if you are patient. The example to the right shows you in a situation with an ace-point game. What do you think your chances of winning are?

Well, in spite of the fact that you

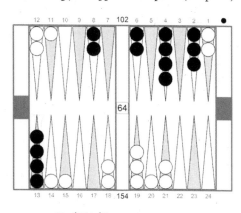

You (White) have an ace-point game.

have a big pip deficit and two checkers stuck at the back, your chance of winning is actually just over 30%. This is because you are highly likely to get at least one shot at Black. He has quite a fragmented situation and is unlikely to get home without exposing checkers to you. If you do hit Black, you have another advantage: timing. You can afford to sit tight and hold that ace-point through quite a number of throws, moving your other checkers around the board and creating a strong home board ready for when you hit him. If Black is foolish enough to offer you a double at this stage, you should welcome it with open arms!

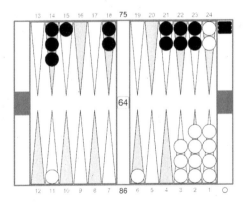

Black still has a 35% chance of winning here.

Poor timing spoils your chances.

Now let's look at the reverse scenario, when your opponent has an ace-point game, i.e. two back-markers on the 1-point in your home board.

On the left, you are ahead in the race; but don't underestimate Black's chances of winning. This scenario is a little extreme because some of your checkers are marooned in your outer board, so you will probably have to leave your opponent a shot at hitting you at least once in order to get all your checkers into the home board. If Black does hit you, he becomes a big favourite to win.

Often the success of an ace-point game depends on **timing**. If your timing is poor and you don't move your backmarkers out before your board starts to crash (i.e. you have had to move your checkers so far along your home board, you are losing your blockade), your chances also plummet.

WHEN TO HIT;
WHEN TO RUN

In the position here, you have two options. You could hit and make your 9-point or you could make your 5-point. You could even bypass the exposed blot (by taking the 1-move first) and go on to make your 9-point without hitting. If you do anything other than hit, your winning chances might be slightly

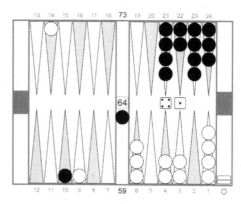

Hit and make your 9-point.

(maybe 1%) higher, but your chances of winning a gammon will plummet by half almost, from 21% to 13%. In this scenario, it is well worth hitting that second checker and making your 9-point.

In the game below, you are winning by a long margin in the race. You have the choice of hitting (by taking the 5-move first) or racing past the exposed black checker on your 11-point. The cube is showing a 2 and is on Black's side, which means that Black has accepted a double from you at an earlier stage in the game. It also means that if you win a gammon, you win 4 points. Even if you hit and are hit back, you are still likely to win the game (and gain 2 points). But if you are lucky enough not to get hit, you have a very strong chance of winning that gammon if you hit Black and put him back even further in the race.

So it makes sense to hit Black with the 5-move first rather than move past him. Also, weigh up how many possibilities there are for you to get hit back on Black's next roll if you *do* hit against and how many possibilities there are for you to get hit if you *don't* hit him. You will see that there is a greater chance of you getting hit if you don't hit him than if you do. Also remember that when you hit your opponent, he must waste part of his next turn simply in re-entering off the bar.

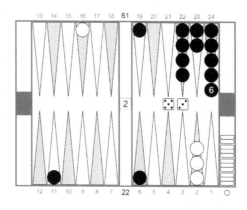

Hit Black by taking the 5-move first, rather than racing past him.

CONTAINMENT

Containment is where you have hit your opponent in the final stages of the game and want to contain his checker within your home board until you have all your checkers in your home board and can safely finish (and hopefully win a gammon). This is not as easy as it sounds!

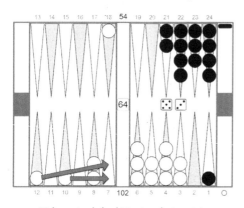

Make a prime before hitting in order to contain Black's last backmarker.

In this next position, you've got two choices: to hit black's blot or to make a 6-point-prime to block him. Blocking makes more sense here because if you let him escape with his 50-pip lead, he's sure to win. Making the 6-point-prime buys you more time. You can then hopefully hit him on your next throw and, with such a strong home board, it will hopefully be a few throws before he manages to re-enter. You contain him until you have caught up with him.

If you take a similar scenario but where you are in the lead, then hitting makes more sense. The aim in the example shown below is to win a race that you are already winning. There is no advantage to containing Black. You can still make your 1-point and put Black on the bar, but there is no need to build that prime to contain him first. Again, there is now a strong chance that Black will not be able to re-enter for a number of throws. This stops him from moving his other checkers and thus increases your chances of winning a gammon.

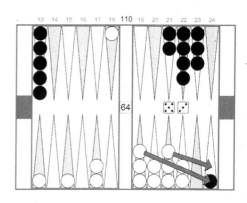

You are in the lead, so you might as well hit.

On the right, with your 6+5 you can hit or block. Hitting (using the checker on your 8-point and then moving one of the checkers on your bar-point in to make your 2-point) is a tempting choice. But after this, if Black threw a joker (in this case a 1+6, allowing him to re-enter and then hit you), you would be finished because he has a 6-point-prime in his home board and you would be unable to continue until he releases points after bearing off (by which

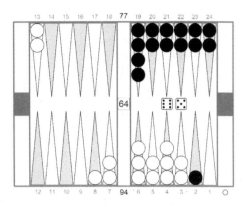

The temptation is to hit, but Black could subsequently throw a joker that would effectively end your game.

point you will be well on your way to losing a gammon). So in this scenario it is better to continue to build the prime.

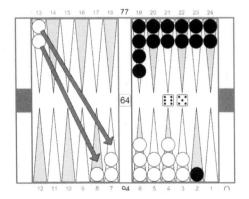

Your best option is to make a 6-point-prime (think of this as a rule of thumb).

The diagram on the left shows what will happen if you build the prime instead of hitting. Now there is no risk of having your chances scuppered by a joker, so you can relax while Black starts to crash his home board (because he cannot move his backmarker until you break up your blockade). I always breathe a little easier when I have a 6-point-prime, so I will generally make one wherever I can, unless there is a very strong reason not to.

WHEN YOU ARE FORCED TO LEAVE A BLOT

If you have to leave a blot in your home board at any point, remember to leave it on the highest point you can, because if your opponent is going to hit you, it's best he isn't too deep in your home board, from where he could hit you again.

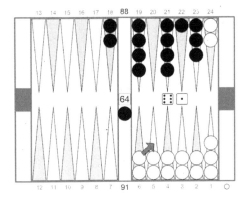

If you have to expose a checker in this scenario, make sure it's the one on the highest point.

In the example on the left, you can't move the 6 because your backmarkers are blocked, but you have a number of choices for your 1-move. The problem is, every choice will leave an exposed blot, so choose one highest up the board. Then, if Black is lucky enough to throw a 6 and hit you, he can't hit further checkers in your home board if you are forced to expose any more of them.

BEARING OFF UNDER FIRE

The expression **bearing off under fire** refers to when you start bearing off while your opponent still has checkers in your home board or is dancing on the bar.

As we've said before, in backgammon it ain't over 'til it's over. Backgammon is *the* game for comeback kings and queens everywhere because there are so many ways in which you can come back from a very poor position indeed – almost from the dead!

Sometimes you can come back because your opponent gives you a chance he shouldn't have. Conversely, don't give your opponent that advantage by giving away any unnecessary shots at hitting you. When bearing off always aim not to have odd numbers of checkers on the higher half of your home board (your 4-point, 5-point and 6-point), reducing the chances that throwing two high numbers would force you to leave a blot exposed.

Backgammon player and author Chris Bray has a great rule of thumb that you should apply to you home board when bearing off under fire. If you can play 6+6 safely, you can usually play anything safely; i.e. if you could make all four 6-moves without a problem, you are likely to be covered. So try to leave your board in that shape for the next move, like this...

If you could play a 6+6 safely, you could play any move safely.

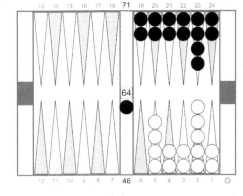

In the example on the right, you are ready to bear off (although you are under fire because Black still has his backmarkers on your ace-point) and you've thrown a 3+3. Although it would be tempting to bear off four checkers with all of your four 3-moves, you can't guarantee that on your next throw you won't have to expose checkers on your higher points. At this stage it's more important to play safely than to push

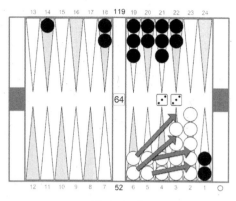

Playing it safe.

for the gammon. It's safer to move your checkers from your 5-point and 6-point and stack them on your 2-point and 3-point from where you can safely start bearing off without leaving exposed blots, rather than rush to bear any checkers off.

Remember, your first priority is to win the game. Only when your victory is pretty much assured should you focus on winning a gammon.

CHOOSE YOUR MOVES CAREFULLY

Be careful not to make silly mistakes in your rush to bear off. At a tournament once I saw the following board and watched White make a disastrous blunder. White could, and should, have moved his highest checker (the one on his 5-point) along one space with his 1-move and then taken it off with his 6-move. Instead he used *the 6-move* to take off the checker on his 5 point and used the 1-move to hit black with checker from his stack on his 2-point. This was a totally unnecessary risk because Black then threw a 1 and was able to hit back, which totally scuppered

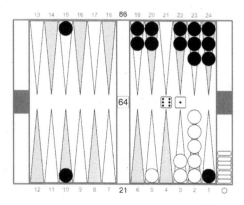

You don't have to bear off the backmarker with the 6-move; you can make the 1-move first followed by the 6-move, which is by far the safer option in this scenario.

White's chance of winning the gammon he was gunning for. I'm convinced everybody watching felt the same 'ouch' as we saw White make the move, but it's easily done in the heat of the moment. **It's important to remember that you don't have to move the highest number first.**

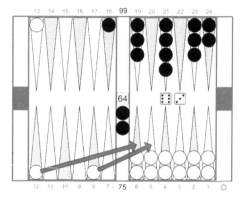

Stack your checkers on the highest points to increase your chances of a gammon.

MAXIMISING YOUR CHANCES OF A GAMMON

In the example on the left, you have a 50% chance of winning a gammon. To maximise the chances of this, stack the remaining checkers on the high numbers if possible, to maximise the value of your throws when bearing off.

THE RACE IS ON

Once you have broken free and there are no more of your opponent's checkers behind yours (and obviously vice versa), you are left in a race. After this stage, the game is usually only played up until the point where someone is winning by enough to offer the next

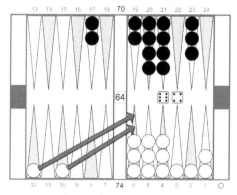

Don't worry about tidiness in a race; just get your checkers into your home board as soon as possible and start bearing off.

double, which the other player will likely decline, forcing the game to end on whatever points it was being played for at this stage.

When you are racing, it's nearly always better to get all your pieces into your home board as quickly as you can. On the left, you might be tempted to use your 6+4 to tidy up your home board rather than having five checkers stacked on your 6-point. However, you don't need a tidy board when you are in a clear race because there is no threat to exposed checkers. Just get everyone home and start bearing off as soon as you can. You never know, you might throw a 6+6 on your next turn and get to bear four of those checkers off. There is no need to worry about tidiness once the race is on.

BEARING-OFF TACTICS

Bearing off is simple, but many people still get it wrong. If you leave unnecessary exposed blots, you can end up completely turning the game against you. You can even lose the game or the chance of a gammon through inefficiency when bearing off. The art of

bearing off efficiently and safely is one of the simplest things you can learn to improve your game.

First of all, it's always best to leave checkers on all six points when you are bearing off, so that you won't waste a throw.

In the example on the right, it's better to use the 5-move to take the checker on your 7-point to your 2-point and then bear off a checker from your 6-point. The other option is to use the 6-move to take your checker on your 7-point to your 1-point and then bear off a checker from your 5-point. If you make the latter choice, you will leave your 2-point empty, and only one checker on your 5-point. So the first option is the best.

Let's look at some more examples of efficient moves once the race is on.

In this next position, you have thrown a 2+3. You have many choices of which checkers to move.

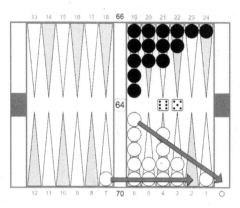

Make the move that allows you to leave checkers on every point, to maximise your chances of bearing off with both moves in your next throw.

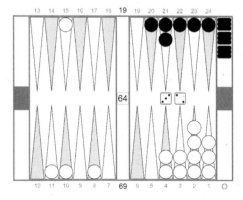

You have many choices with your 3+2.

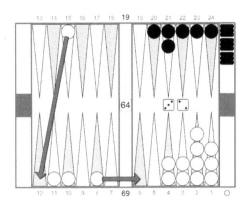

Moving for maximum efficiency.

Your priority in this scenario is to save yourself from losing a gammon. Moving your further checker onto your 12-point and moving the checker on your 8-point into your home board will give you around a 50% chance of saving yourself from being gammoned. If you make any other move, your chances of saving yourself from being gammoned drop to as low as 33%. That's a big difference.

Efficiency means not wasting any spaces. When you are in the position of saving yourself from being gammoned, always look at whether you can move a checker onto your 6-point. Don't worry about moving in any further than that. With any remaining moves, first look at any that will allow a checker to 'cross over' from one quadrant to the next, and then focus on bringing the checkers in your outer board closer to home. A good rule of thumb for when you can't move any checker into your home board or 'cross over', is simply to move the checker that is farthest away from home.

WHEN TO DOUBLE IN THE FINAL RACE

It is a basic rule that you should ask yourself whether or not to offer a double before *every* turn. Never is this more important than in the final stages of a race. The **10% doubling rule** is a quick way of assessing your position in a race. Whenever it is your throw, if you add 10% to your pip count and this doesn't put you more than two pips ahead, you should double. As long as your opponent has a pip count that is 2 points or more than you, he should take the double.

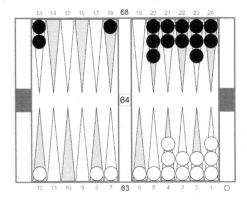

The 10% doubling rule says you should
offer the double.

In the example above, it is your turn and you have a pip count of 63 versus Black's 68. Adding 10% to your total makes it 69.3; this is not more than two higher than Black, so you should offer the double.

Estimating the pip count to assess a numerical lead works pretty well in the normal course of play. However, once you start racing your proximity to the finishing line distorts the relevance of the pip count. In the example below, both players are on a pip count of 48, but a number of factors mean that you have a huge advantage over Black. It's your turn, which gives you a percentage lead of around 10%. Also, Black has more checkers to bear off and even though they are on low points, he has some gaps in his home board, which will make him more likely to waste throws.

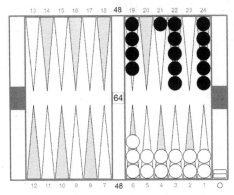

Although you are on equal pips, you clearly have an
advantage so you should offer the double.

You should offer the double,
but Black should not accept.

In the similar example on the right, your total pip count is 48 compared to his 47, so it is less than four higher than Black and you should double. Because Black is less than two pips ahead, he should not take your double.

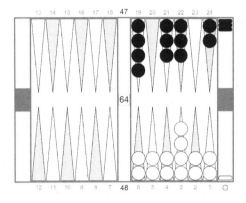

AN UNSPORTING ENDGAME TRICK

Here's an old ruse to watch out for. Often it is considered good sporting manners for the losing player to concede the rest of a game during the final stages of a race, when all hope is lost. There's nothing wrong with that. But a losing player still has to race his last few checkers home and bear one off to avoid a gammon. Watch out for an experienced player 'sportingly' conceding to you a single game to 'save time' when in fact he was struggling to bear off a checker. By accepting you might have thrown away your chance to win a gammon had you played on. This happened to me a few times before it dawned on me that I'd been tricked out of an extra point. A good rule of thumb is, don't accept a losing player conceding a game until they've borne off at least one checker and you know that the gammon is off the cards. Obviously I am not suggesting you use this ruse yourself on inexperienced players...!

Now there's an expensive game... a giant board display in Asprey
on London's Bond Street.

PART III

HOW TO

START WINNING

Liberace

©Las Vegas Backgammon Magazine

10

ALWAYS HAVE A
GAME PLAN

*At every stage of the game you should
constantly be evaluating and updating your
game plan. To have no plan at all will
leave you lost on the back roads
of mediocrity forever.*

KENT GOULDING

I DIDN'T HAVE MUCH OF A PLAN...

a s I walked up the steps of a private members club in St James's in London. The place reeked of tradition and it didn't look as though anything had been touched over the couple of centuries since it first opened its doors. There were no women around; presumably the only females who ever saw the inside of this building were those hired to cook and clean. The first thing I noticed was that everyone was wearing a dinner jacket and bow tie; everyone except me. I had to make a split-second decision. The pre-tournament dinner was due to start in 30 minutes. Should I turn around, go home, get changed, find a bow tie, while the taxi meter clocked up a fortune, and then return to the club and arrive at the dinner late? Or should I sweat out the whole evening in the wrong clothes – a blue suit with a pink tie – looking like a character in a H.M. Bateman cartoon? I couldn't face the latter, so I raced home, got changed and come back in a funk... but also in a bow tie and a dinner jacket, hastily borrowed from a neighbour whose shoulders were roughly twice the width of mine.

Always have a plan, Stan... and a black tie.

As I walked into the lounge and saw the backgammon tables scattered around the elegant room, I began to wonder if I really belonged in this place. The members all seemed supremely self-confident and acted as though they'd all known each other from birth. My shirt collar felt tight and I was sure I was the only one who was sweating profusely. I looked around for my host but I couldn't see him.

At last someone turned and looked at me as if he knew me. He was unfamiliar to me but he walked over, smiling. I thought maybe I knew him from somewhere. What a relief to see a friendly face. But before I could put out my hand to shake his, the man promptly asked me to bring him two large vodka tonics and a glass of white wine.

ALWAYS HAVE A GAME PLAN: RUN, HIT OR PRIME

There is a delicious point in the process of learning anything complicated when the mist rises, like in the film *The Matrix* when the hero, Neo, suddenly figures out how to read the code.

Before we talk about some specific winning moves of backgammon, you need to drill a fundamental principle into your head. Applying this principle alone will enable you to beat most people most of the time, simply because they, themselves, don't apply it with enough rigour, if at all. I've already mentioned it several times in this book, but now I want to devote a whole chapter to it because without it, you really have no chance of getting good at backgammon. The rule is: **always have a game plan**!

You always, always, *always* need to **have a plan in your mind**, every time you play a move. That plan should be relevant to your current situation. Of course your plan can change as the game continues, depending on where you stand, but you must always replace it with a different plan. **At every stage in the game you must always be clear on what your plan is**.

That might sound daunting, but here's the good news: despite the trillions of potential positions and decisions there are in every game of backgammon, there are only **three plans** you can have. If you **always** have one of those plans in your mind before every move you make, your game will develop beautifully and you will soon become a class backgammon act. If you don't, you won't.

These three game plans are: **run**, **hit** or **prime**. Keep all three in your mind at all times and know which one you are following at any given moment, because the moves you make need to be consistent with your current plan. Your game plan can, and will, change several times through a single game, and even from one move to the next, but following this mantra – of always knowing which game plan you are following as you take each move – will allow you to read the moves in each game more clearly.

Over the course of my playing I've discovered that if I think about my game plan first and *then* consider each possible move, trying to make a move that best supports that game plan, even if I don't select the best move I will avoid making a blunder. Most of my blunders have occurred when I haven't had a specific game plan in mind before making a move.

1) Running (racing)

Backgammon professional Neil Kasaross once said, 'I win so many games because I'm ahead in the race, it's shocking. People just think I'm lucky, but I always want to be ahead in the race almost no matter what.' Neil makes a very good point here. Sometimes the best plan is to run. Too many players forget that they are in a race. As a general rule, if you have less pips remaining than your opponent, you should usually be racing around the board and hoping to finish first. If you're winning by more than a few pips and you can keep going without being blocked or hit, you will win the game more often than you will lose it by running. A novice has a better chance of beating a champion with this game plan, so this is a great strategy if you're playing against a more experienced player.

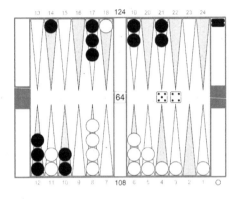

White has thrown 5+4. Should you hit or run?

On the left, you have thrown 5+4. Since you are winning in the race and you just have one checker lagging behind, it makes sense to move that last checker to catch up with the rest (to go with the game plan of running). However, having decided to run, you still have two choices: you could hit Black with the 4-move then continue around the board with the 5-move, or you could move the 5-move first, then the 4-move, thus arriving at the same place but avoiding hitting Black.

You are not very likely to win a gammon by capturing just one piece, and you're clearly ahead in the race by a decent number of pips, so there really isn't any point in hanging around. Plus you have three exposed

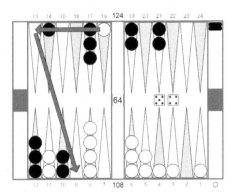

Here, it is better to skip the hit and just run.

blots in your home board, so you would be extremely vulnerable if you hit Black.

As much fun as hitting is, in this scenario, because you are ahead in the race and your game plan at this point in the game is **running** (and because your home board is so vulnerable) you should skip past the Black checker and run, as shown in the diagram to the left. Never forget that backgammon is a race.

2) Hitting

Hitting is often a great game plan, and one that gives you a number of advantages. Firstly it puts you further ahead in the race simply because your opponent's checker has to start again. It also gives you more opportunities to trap your opponent in your home board. Finally, it limits your opponent's choices with his next throw because one of his moves must be to re-enter the game with his checker – if he can do so at all.

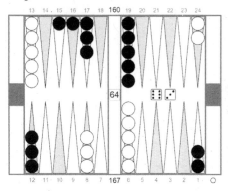

Your best game plan is hitting here; hit Black
with one of your backmarkers.

Above, you have an obvious hitting opportunity. Once you hit Black on your 16-point, he will have three checkers stuck back in your home area. He also has to waste at least one of his two dice in the next throw in order to re-enter the game. Plus his pip count has gone up due to the fact that the checker that was hit has to start again. It's clearly a good idea for you to hit at this stage.

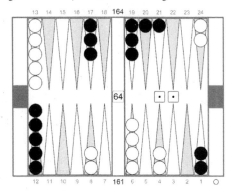

To hit or to prime?

In the example on the left, you (White) have had the luck of throwing a 1+1 early on in the game.

You've got some great choices here. Making a prime is definitely a good idea, especially as Black has two checkers stuck in your home board. So you could make a 4-point-prime (by moving two checkers from your 6-point to make your 5-point, as well as moving the two checkers on your

8-point to your bar-point). This is not a bad choice at all. However, in this scenario, it's actually a better move to hit (as shown on the left), because you can hit twice. While your opponent is struggling to get back on the board (chances are it will take him a couple of goes because you are blocking him with your 4-point and 6-point) you can make progress, running those checkers even further around or changing your game plan and adding to your prime.

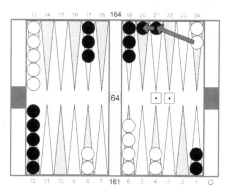

Your best game plan is hitting, so hit Black twice.

At this exact stage of the game, hitting is the best game plan because it buys you time and uses up some, or all, of your opponent's next throw. A tactic worth remembering.

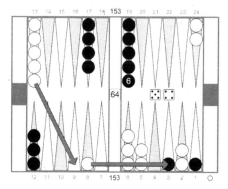

Hit, and hope for the best because it's too early to race.

Sometimes it's a good idea to hit simply because it's too early on in the game to run. In the example shown on the left, both players are on 153 pips and White's two backmarkers have not even started to move, so it is a little early in the game to pick running as your game plan. Priming also seems an unsuitable game plan at this stage because Black has split his backmarkers and you have very few anchors – or even builders – outside your home board. But you do have three points in your home board and Black has two blots, thus hitting is the best game plan.

When you have made **more home board points than your opponent**, this tells you that you have a real advantage in a hitting game. In the example above, Black only has one home board point while you have three. If the hitting goes back and forth, Black is more likely to be left dancing on the bar because he has fewer options for re-entering than you have, due to the fact that you are blocking him with your three points.

By a process of elimination we discovered that our best game plan here is to hit. However, it is still early on in the game, so once you have congratulated yourself for spotting the right game plan, you need to pause and consider your next question: which hit is best? Technically, you can hit either of Black's blots in your home board. If you hit Black's furthest backmarker (on your 1-point), you won't be able to cover the blot you leave on your next turn with a single dice (you would require a 7 or a 12 but you only have a 5). So it's best to hit Black's blot on your 3-point as you then have a better chance of covering it by using the builder on your 6-point if you throw a 3 in your next roll.

Once you've hit Black's checker on your 3-point with your 5-move, you still need to move the remaining 4. Remember, your current game plan is hitting. To follow this you need to try to cover the blot you have now left on point 3 in your home board. To do this, you make your 4-move by taking a checker from your midpoint to your 9-point. Now you have a second chance of covering the blot you left on your next throw because if you throw a 6, you can cover it using that blot you left on your 9-point.

At this stage of the game, with 3 points in your home board, there is also the possibility that neither of Black's dice will work for him and he will have to dance on the bar thus wasting at least one entire throw. With the pip count so evenly matched, this alone could give you a substantial lead. Of course, Black might throw a 3 and hit you as he re-enters, but no one said backgammon was risk free!

3) Priming

Building primes can be a great game plan. There is nothing more delicious in backgammon than holding a 6-point-prime and watching your opponent's game crumble because he can't get past it no matter what he throws. Indeed, building a 6-point-prime in front of your opponent's backmarkers is the most pain you can inflict on him!

The first step in your ultimate goal of building a 6-point-prime is to start making points as close together as you can. This is a way of gaining territory. It also makes it easier for you to transport your other checkers around the board because they can land on your points, and harder for your opponent to do so because he can't land on them.

I said prime, not primate.

David Teniers the Younger

Priming is the spice of backgammon. Always be on the lookout for a good opportunity to block your opponent by building a strong prime. Playing a priming game plan is what is called 'playing pure backgammon'. Good players are always trying to make their points close together and not to make the 1-point or 2-point too early unless the situation forces them to do so. Building the points in the middle and left of the home board first gives you a better chance of building that ultimate 6-point-prime because you have space either side to add to it and make small primes as you work your way up to 6. You are much more likely to get to a 5-point-prime or 6-point-prime by doing this.

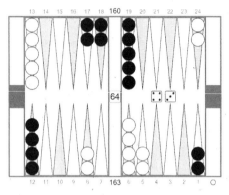

Look for the best move.

In the example above, both players have had good first throws, and made good use of them by making points and starting to build primes. Now White has thrown a 4+3, which is not such a tidy throw. It might be tempting to play safe by moving one checker from the midpoint into the home board. This move certainly has something going for it in that it's safe in the short-term and it moves a checker into the home board. However, as always, it pays to look again to see if there is a better move.

In this case, there are actually four better moves, even though each one exposes two checkers. You could move both your backmarkers to leave two blots in your opponent's home board (with the intention of making an anchor there, perhaps) or you could move two checkers from your mid-point and slot your 10-point and 9-point. You could also move one each of your backmarkers and midmarkers, and there are two possible ways to do this (use the 3-move to move the backmarker and the 4-move to move the midmarker, or vice versa).

In all of these alternate moves you are achieving a lot more than the safer play of using both moves to take one of your midmarkers to your 6-point, because you are setting up great builders on which to make points.

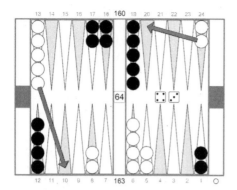

Move one from the back and one from the middle.

Technically, the best move is to move the backmarker with your 4-move and the midmarker with your 3-move. As shown in the diagram above, this creates a priming opportunity as well as giving you the chance to make your opponent's 5-point.

This example was somewhat complex, but it makes a great point: always consider all the different moves you could make. Too often a player might see a great move and take it too hastily, missing an even better one.

The great player Kit Woolsey once said, 'Many, possibly most, inferior moves are made not because the best play was considered and then rejected, but because the best play was completely overlooked.'

WORKING OUT THE BEST GAME PLAN

We are going to look at two scenarios where you have to play a 6+5 halfway through a game.

In the first scenario, shown on the right, your board looks quite tidy and you have a strong 3-point-prime in your home quarter. However, you are losing the race by 38 pips (your opponent has 94 pips to go and you have 132 pips to go). This is a big lead for Black at this stage and as it's a race, you're almost certainly going to lose. So while it looks tempting and neat to move your two backmarkers and

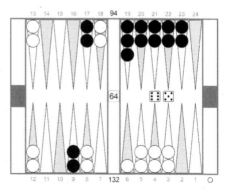

White has thrown a 6+5.

neatly slot them onto your 13-point and 14-point, this would be a mistake because you are actually helping to move the race along... a race you are on course to lose.

So in this scenario, racing is not your best game plan. You would be better off moving your more advanced checkers off the 12-point (as shown on the right) to make your 6-point and slot your bar-point. Now you have a 4-point-prime and a chance of making a 6-point-prime. This also enables you

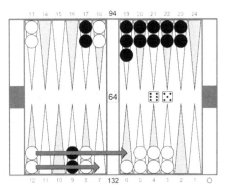

Your game plan should be priming here. Move your two checkers from the 12-point to continue adding to your prime; don't move your backmarkers.

to continue to hold a double threat against your opponent from your mid-point and your anchor on Black's bar-point. Black is now faced with the tricky task of moving his two backmarkers around the board without you hitting them.

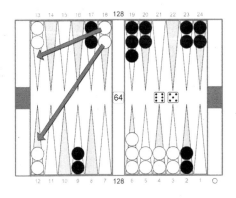

This time your game plan is to run so you should safely move your two backmarkers.

Now let's look at a second scenario where your checkers are in a similar position to the example above, but your opponent is at a very different stage. In this example you have a much better chance of winning in a straight race because your pip count is the same as your opponent's (you're both on 128). Black also has two checkers stuck behind your 4-point-prime in your home board.

In this case it *is* a good idea to release your anchor and get your back-markers onto your 12-point and 13-point with your throw of 6+5. You are now winning the race. Here you played with a **running game plan** and will probably continue to do so. Even though you might encounter some difficult scenarios ahead of you, there's no doubt that playing these moves with your throw of 6+5 has helped you to move things along; it would have been a mistake to hang back.

So there you have the three game plans: **run, hit** and **prime**. Keep them in your mind at all times. The moves you choose need to be consistent with the game plan you are playing at every stage of the game. You can, and should, change your game plan several times in a single game, and even from roll to roll. But the most important thing is **to have a game plan at all times**.

If you can't decide what your game plan should to be at any particular stage, take a look at your opponent's game plan and oppose it. If, for example, your opponent is playing a running game, try to stop him with either a hitting or priming game. If it looks like your opponent is trying to prime, you need to run with those backmarkers even if you have to split them, so that they won't get stuck. You can also using hitting as a strategy to hold your opponent up. Having said that, you can also beat him at his own game plan if that seems to be your best option. For example, you can make a prime of your own to counterbalance a prime your opponent is clearly working on. Ordinarily, you should obviously choose a game plan that is based on your position and the numbers on the dice, but don't shy away from choosing a retaliating game plan – choosing a game plan simply because it will stop your opponent from succeeding with his own.

Clarke Gable and Claudette Colbert

11

TACTICAL PLAY

In the short run, there are no guarantees.
You may become an excellent player and still
lose a 100-point session to a clod, or get knocked
out in the first round of six consecutive tournaments,
or reach the final of the biggest tournament of
your life and lose 0-25. Those are the breaks.
If you can' t handle that much uncertainty,
tough, go play chess.

BILL ROBERTIE
(TWO TIMES BACKGAMMON WORLD CHAMPION)

TACTICS OR 'TACTICS'

Tactics are skilful ways in which you can maximise your chances of winning. They are all things you can do that fall within the rules of the game. Occasionally you might come across a player who takes matters a step further.

'I've drawn our old buddy Max in the next round,' Will told me sourly. It wasn't that Max, a veteran of the backgammon circuit, was likely to beat Will, it was the process with which he would probably do it. Will knew that he would end up gently correcting the 'accidental' moves with a weary smile. Max would 'accidentally' move 5 checkers instead of 4 after throwing a double, occasionally even moving 6 checkers. Sometimes he would move a checker that convenient one space too many to reach safety. He had been known to bear off counters at such speed that he managed to bear off an extra one. He had even been caught slightly adjusting the scoring pad in his favour with a slip of the pen.

'It's just so tiring and humiliating correcting him,' Will complained. 'He's been playing 40 years longer than me. And he doesn't take criticism well; he growls. The whole thing is so embarrassing.'

I didn't have any helpful advice for Will. All I could say was, 'There's a Max in every area of life; did you imagine backgammon would be any different?'

I've heard other stories of players who will use a certain amount of sleight of hand, and even loaded or biased dice, but these stories are few and far between. The only case I know of that took place in a major competition was when Falafel was accused of 'stealing a pip' by Danish professional Sander Lylloff in a tight game in the Nordic Open. This is where a player in a close race to the finish 'accidentally' moves one point more than his dice actually allow. But the most outrageous form of cheating that goes on in backgammon is in online play where you can't see your opponent, as we will see in the chapter 'Playing for real.'

PLAYING WITH TACTICS

It's important to **think tactically** when you play. Too often, inexperienced players will sleepwalk through a game and lose simply because their opponent was more thoughtful.

Let's go back to basics and start by thinking about the **opening position**.

At the beginning of the game, it's important to think about how you are going to start **dissolving the stacks**, the 10 out of your 15 checkers that make up two big piles of 5 checkers each. One is at the halfway point and the other is in your home board.

It's a good idea to dissolve these

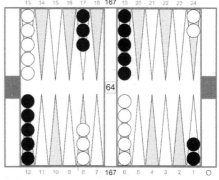

The opening position.

stacks early on and use your checkers to create **points** and **primes**. This will help you to block your opponent's path home and smooth your own journey. If you can't use your checkers early on in the game to make points, at least move them individually so that they can help you make points later.

Most beginners try to play too safely at the start. They keep stacking their checkers up for fear of getting hit. Stacking your checkers together will give you less safe places to move to in later moves and thus leave you more exposed to being hit later on in the game, when it hurts much more. In the early stages of the game you should be taking more chances, before your opponent has had the chance to make some points on his side of the board.

Try to shift your **two backmarkers** around the board early on in the game, because it won't be much fun trying to do so later on.

At the same time as focusing on these tactical priorities yourself, you should also be thinking about how to **stop your opponent** from making these tactical moves himself.

DON'T LEAN BACK

The great early twentieth-century American cartoonist James Thurber said, 'You might as well fall flat on your face as lean too far backwards.'

When you're skiing it feels right to lean back, into the mountain; it feels safe. However, it is safer to lean forward and away from the mountain. All good skiers know this; even bad skiers like me know it. So why do we all lean back when we first learn to ski? Because we're afraid of the slope or the speed we're building. The same applies in backgammon. Inexperienced players 'lean back', trying to play safely, when they should actually be playing a bit more aggressively. Novices often think they have a better chance of winning by racing around the board unimpeded, praying that their luck will hold out; but this rarely happens. Or they will be constantly looking to play safe moves that don't leave any exposed blots; in the short run this feels safer, but it can trip you up later.

I thought you said lean back?

It's always better to **play aggressively** than safely. Of course if you overdo it the recklessness will cost you dearly, but, on the whole, beginners tend to play far too timidly and could improve their chances if they were willing to take a few more risks. As the great player Phil Simborg says, 'Sometimes the greatest risk is to take no risk at all.'

Remember, getting hit is not the end of the world – in fact, it's far from it. When it happens early on in a game, it can even work to your advantage. For example, while it might slow you down in a race that you are already losing, you can often use the checker to hit your opponent back when you re-enter the game – sometimes in his home board, which is particularly painful for him and will even up the pip count again. You could even hit one of his checkers when he is in the middle of bearing off. Then he would need to re-enter his checker in your home board and he could be blocked from doing so on a number of points, which would mean he has to skip one or more turns. This would allow you to catch up. Being hit sometimes turns the tables completely and gives you a real chance of winning in a game you had almost written off. So, never assume it's the end of the world if you're hit. It could actually work to your advantage.

ARE YOU PLAYING TOO SAFELY?

There are often some tell-tale signs that you are playing too safely. If you have a stack of checkers in one place, not only does it look messy, but it's also a sign that you have been prioritising safe play over good tactical play.

In the example to the right, you (White), have used your first few throws, some of which added up to 7, to safely move your checkers onto your 6-point. After this move of 4+3, you have no less than 9 checkers on your 6-point. As a result of this imbalanced board, you will struggle to contain Black and to get your own remaining checkers around the board without problems. Black is in fact already statistically favourite to win from here.

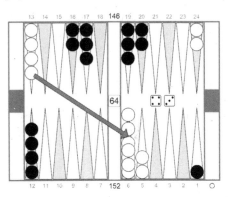

White lacks balance.

CREATING OBSTACLES

Your opponent will be trying to put up obstacles by building primes. You should do the same. You can also use these primes as vital stepping-stones to help your other checkers move around the board.

Try to think of your home board as a fortress. You need to build walls to keep your opponent out and ease your own way home. The key building blocks are your 5-point, your 4-point and your bar-point (remember you begin the game with a wall on your 6-point so you already have this covered.)

In the game to the right, you have made your bar-point, your 5-point

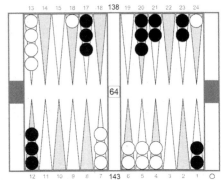

White is building a fortress.

and your 4-point. As a result you have a very useful 4-point-prime. Black has also made some points but his are more spread out and that's why White is the strong favourite to win at this stage in this particular game. Obviously, your ultimate aim is to build a **six-point-prime**. You will be hard to beat if Black is trapped behind a six-point prime.

In order to make these points, you have to take chances by **slotting** them first (i.e. leaving a blot on the point even though it might get hit). If you're lucky and your blot doesn't get hit, you will hopefully be able to land on the blot with your next throw, make the point and reap the subsequent rewards. Like everything in this game, you are always weighing the risks against the rewards. In the early stages of the game the rewards of making points outweigh the risks of getting hit, so slot away!

WHY IS THE 5-POINT SO IMPORTANT?

Philip Martyn, a leading writer and player in the 1970s, believed that the 'most important points on the board are the two 5-points (yours and your opponent's).'

Making a point on your own 5-point or your opponent's is a good idea, but making both is nirvana and gets you into a great position.

Making your own 5-point is important because it makes it more difficult for your opponent to free his backmarkers. It also serves as a safe landing site for your own checkers when you are bringing the game home. **Making your opponent's 5-point** hampers his efforts to bring his checkers home and finish the game. When you hold a high point in your opponent's home board, it makes it risky for him to leave blots in his outer board because you could so easily hit them with one of the checkers on your point. The less flexibility you give your opponent to bring his checkers home, the better.

The 7-point and the 4-point are also pretty good, though strategically not quite as wonderful as the

Philip Martyn

5-point. The 6-point is, of course, already occupied from the start and generally remains occupied. Having home-board points is also important for reducing your opponent's chances for re-entering the game when you hit him, so making any of your home-board points is a good idea, but the 5-point is slightly stronger because it is next to your 6-point and therefore builds a 2-point-prime.

CHOOSING TO MAKE YOUR OPPONENT'S 5-POINT

In the example shown to your right, you have a rather nice throw of 4+3 and can choose from a couple of excellent options. You could make your own 4-point quite neatly or you could make your opponent's 5-point. If you make your 4-point, you will start to build your home board. However, Black has already freed one of his two backmarkers so it's too late to realise the full value of doing this. Also, look out for all the Black checkers looming towards Black's home board where they might trap your two White backmarkers that are still stuck there.

In my opinion, in this scenario it would be better for you to make Black's 5-point. By doing so, you spoil Black's chances of trapping you (as shown on the right, middle).

CHOOSING TO MAKE YOUR OWN 5-POINT

In this next position you have thrown a 6+4 and have several options. You could move both of your backmarkers and neatly cover your two blots that are sitting in Black's outer board. That's not a bad idea but it commits you to racing

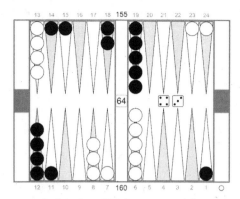

Spoilt for choice. With this 4+3 you can either make Black's 5-point or your own 4-point.

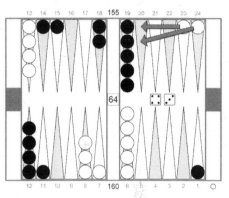

White decides to make a 5-point in Black's home board.

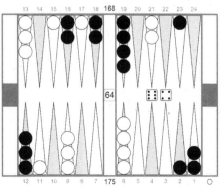

You have a couple of strong choices. Will you cover your blots or move them forward, or make your 5-point?

to the finish, which is risky at this stage because after this move you will only be 3 pips ahead of Black (165 for you versus 168 for Black) and he would have the additional advantage of it being his throw.

Alternatively, you could move those two blots forward neatly so that they land together, covering the third blot and making your 11-point. You could also make your bar-point (by moving the blot on your 11-point with your 4-move and one of your midmarkers with your 6-move), giving you a 2-point-prime. However, neither of these moves is as good as making your 5-point (by moving a checker off your 9-point and the blot off your 11-point). This also gives you a 2-point-prime, but in an even stronger position. The fact that Black has 3 checkers stuck at the back means that priming is a good game plan.

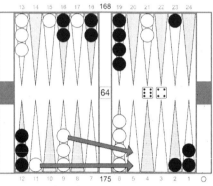

You (White) make your 5-point despite other strong choices.

I hope, by now, I have stressed how important the 5-point is. I am a huge fan of the 5-point, as are many good players. Paul Magriel, one of the greatest backgammon players of all time, even called the 5-point the **golden point**.

The great Paul Magriel, 1978 World Champion. Like so many of the top players, Paul is also a mathematics professor (despite the fact that he looks pretty cool!)

THE BAR-POINT

The next most useful point after the 5-point, strategically speaking, is the bar-point (the 7-point). Even though it is not actually in your home board (which means it's not as useful when it comes to bearing off), the bar-point has great anchoring and blocking potential.

Your opponent's bar point is also great for blocking. The only disadvantage to holding your opponent's bar-point as opposed to his 5-point is that you can't use it as a landing place to re-enter on if you get hit. Even so, holding your opponent's bar-point is still very useful in preventing your opponent from building a strong prime to trap you. It also serves as a launch pad from which to start racing your checkers home when the time feels right.

In the example shown on the right, you (White) have thrown 6+1. You have the choice of making your bar-point or of moving one of your backmarkers safely onto the midpoint.

It's really too early to race and relinquish the useful anchor you hold on Black's 5-point while leaving one remaining checker stranded there, so making the bar-point is the way to go, as shown on the right. You also make a very strong 5-point-prime by making this move.

When you hold three or more points in your home board, you're usually in a very exciting position, especially if your opponent still has checkers stuck at the back. Even if he doesn't, it will mean your opponent will be afraid of being hit because if he is, his chances of re-entering are reduced. This would allow you to make further progress while he dances on the bar.

THE 4-POINT

The 4-point is also very useful. In the game to the right, which is in its early stages, you have already made Black's 4-point and you've now thrown a 4+2 so you are able to make your own 4-point as well.

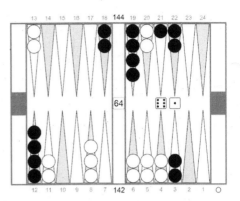

Should you move one of your backmarkers or make your bar-point?

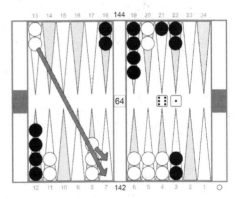

Make your bar-point.

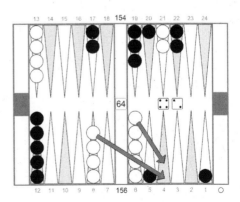

With your 4+2 you make your own 4-point.

BALANCE

We've already discussed how you can rapidly reduce your chances of winning by creating an unbalanced board. *Always* think about **balance**. Balance is a key element of your tactical play. If you rush ahead, leaving your backmarkers behind, you will have a devil of a job getting them out. Temper your aggression with common sense, keep your board evenly spread, and balance your offence and defence, so if you do attack you have some defences against a counter-attack.

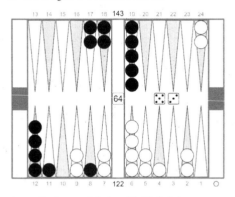

You have created a board that lacks balance.

On the left, you (White) have made a fast start thanks to a 6+6 and a 4+4 but you've neglected to move your backmarkers and Black already has a 3-point-prime. You are going to struggle to get your backmarkers out. Even though Black is currently 21 pips behind, he is now a strong favourite to win the game because of your lack of balance.

Another way to put it is that White has no 'connectivity'. There is no link, such as the presence of midmarkers, to keep a connection with your backmarkers, and they are in danger of becoming trapped and isolated. It's no good having almost all of your checkers ready to bear off because they can't start doing that until any stragglers have joined them. Remember, **the army marches to the pace of the slowest man**!

WHEN IT'S A GOOD IDEA TO HIT

An advantage of hitting your opponent at any stage is that you at least tie up half his throw as he uses up one number just to re-enter in the board. There is even the possibility that he is unable to re-enter the board and has to miss a turn, or even (if he is exceptionally unlucky) several turns. It's a good general rule that, in the early stages of the game, if you have a choice between hitting your opponent on his side of the board, making a point or hitting on your own side of the board, the hit on your opponent's side of the board is probably best because his pip count increases more the further advanced the hit checker was. If you're not sure whether to hit or not it's usually a better move to hit because most of us are too cautious in our calculation of the position. As I've said before, **when in doubt... hit**!

WHEN IT'S NOT A GOOD IDEA TO HIT

Here you've thrown a 1+1, enabling you to re-enter your checker. Using the rest of your 1s you could hit both the blot in Black's home board and the one in your own home board. Hitting *two* of Black's checkers sounds tempting, and hitting the checker in his home board is going to seriously push up his pip count, but it's actually much better here to use the rest of your moves to create a perfect 6-prime (as shown below). You then have plenty of time to hit Black later, because he isn't going anywhere until you let his back-marker out.

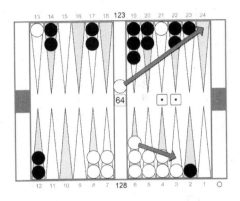

So, hitting Black here is *not* a good idea.

You (White) play it safe and complete your prime.

MOVING YOUR BACKMARKERS OUT

Always look for opportunities to move those backmarkers out, even if you can't take them to safety in one throw. Unless your throw is particularly fortunate (a series of doubles that allow you to move them together) you usually have to take some chances to release your backmarkers. Don't race them ahead so far that you lose opportunities to use them to hit your opponent when he gives you the chance, but avoid allowing them to remain isolated and trapped at the back as the game progresses.

WHEN TO BUILD A PRIME

It's never too early to start building a prime. By making any of the points around your home board you are starting this process. Even if you can't complete a point, you can leave builders. It's often worth sacrificing some safety now for creating an excellent prime later.

A FINAL TACTICAL THOUGHT

To err is human but to miss a better move is just plain dumb...

In other words, considering carefully which is the best play and then making the wrong decision is much more forgivable in backgammon than simply not looking hard enough and missing the right play; one that you would have recognised if you'd looked harder. If you make wrong decisions, that's fine and understandable, they will gradually get better the more you play, but if you don't even look hard enough at the different options, you'll struggle. Backgammon is not a game that is best played too quickly. So even if it's exciting, try to slow it down. **Always consider *all* of your options!**

Douglas Fairbanks, Jr. and Joan Crawford at their home in 1931
using a scoring dial (an early version of the doubling cube).

12

DOUBLE
THE TROUBLE

*I can hardly over-emphasise the
importance of the cube and its influence on play.
Handling the cube correctly is a major part of
backgammon, it must be since it determinates
the end of eighty percent of all games.*

JOE DWEK
(FORMER BACKGAMMON WORLD CHAMPION)

We had a briefing from Nick, our team captain, before our big match against the MCC who, not content with being the world headquarters for cricket, were also top of our London league at backgammon. Nick talked mainly about the practical logistics of the match and added only one piece of playing advice for the team. 'Please be extra careful out there with the doubling cube,' he urged us. Nick knew from (probably bitter) experience that if just one player used the doubling cube unwisely it could throw our chances of victory.

Each of my three matches left me with a different, but familiar, feeling. After the first match (which I lost), I was thinking, 'I played well, he was lucky at the end.' In the second match (which I also lost), I changed the tune in my head to, 'Life is so unfair.' When I finally won a match (with a considerable amount of luck), my ego was shouting, 'I was obviously better than him and I deserved to win all along!'

We won that competition by one point. I didn't contribute much to the overall result, but I did heed Nick's sensible advice. I avoided using the cube too freely.

In golf there is a great saying that goes, 'You drive for show, but you putt for dough.' There is a parallel to this in backgammon. Your checker play is important but often the real money (or victory) is won or lost over the use or misuse of the doubling cube.

The champion backgammon player Kit Woolsey says, 'A player who is savvy with the cube will have an advantage over an opponent who moves the checkers slightly better but makes inferior cube decisions. Thus, it is vital to understand cube decisions in order to be a winning backgammon player.' Players the world over **underestimate the importance of being able to use the doubling cube competently**. And Kent Goulding says, 'Every turn is a new cube decision. Always. Never forget. The biggest error you can make is to fail to double at the appropriate time.' Hank Youngerman adds, 'Trying to play backgammon without the doubling cube is like trying to drive a car without understanding how to turn the steering wheel.'

However, many players *do* forget the vital role the doubling cube plays. Former world champion Tim Holland wrote a book of more than 200 pages on playing backgammon with barely a mention of doubling.

Tim Holland's book from the 1970s.

There are just two questions you need to know the answer to as every game progresses: **when to accept a double** and **when to offer a double.** Your answers to these questions will determine much of your success in the game.

MATCH EQUITY

To make good doubling decisions, you must get to grips with how to calculate or at least estimate what your match equity is at any point in the game. That means your percentage chance of winning the game from that point. (A simple way of understanding this is to think, if you played 100 games that were identical up to the point at which you are calculating your equity, how many would you statistically go on to win after that point? If the answer is 50, your match equity at that point is 50%. If it was 36, your match equity at that stage is 36% etc. You can sometimes work this out exactly in practice, especially as you get very close to finishing, as we will show later.

WHEN SHOULD YOU ACCEPT A DOUBLE?

There is a great question you can ask yourself to help you work out whether or not to accept a double. If you feel your chance of winning the game is more than 25%, you should accept the double. Many people would assume that this figure should be 50%. Instinctively it feels wrong to agree to up the stakes if you are losing at all. You may feel that to accept a double when you are losing by any degree would be madness. However, there is a reason why your **take point** should actually be 25%. I will explain this reason anon.

Remember, your opponent will offer the double when he feels he is ahead in the game and assumes he will win. But don't make a decision until you have really worked out your chances. If you can see that just a little bit of luck could turn the game in your favour, take the risk and keep playing. Remember, if you win, *you* get double the points.

Plus you are in control of the cube, which means you can double back and win even more points if your opponent accepts.

Don't worry if a doubling decision proves costly in the short run; the dice can be cruel. Statistically, accepting the double when you still have a more than 25% chance of winning will work out in your favour once luck and bad luck cancel each other out.

This 25% threshold is approximate (and is worked out before factoring in the possibility of gammons, the match score, the value in holding the cube and other possibilities), but it does stand up to mathematical testing. If you always accept a double when you have a 25% chance of winning a game at the time it is offered, you will, on average, come out ahead.

How can that be when logically it feels as though the figure should be closer to 50%?

Here's the explanation. If you aren't keen on maths, just trust me on this and skip along. Imagine you could play four games that were identical games up to the stage where you were offered a double, and at that stage you had a 25% chance of winning. If you refused the double offer all four times, you would definitely lose 4 points. If you *accepted* the double offer all four times, the odds say that you will win one of those four games (you have a 25% chance, remember). This game is worth 2 points. The *other* three games you would lose (if you accepted all four times) would lose you a total of 6 points. Thus your net loss will be 4 points. This is exactly the same as if you had refused the offer all four times. Thus, when you are at 25% you are at a break-even point. Statistically, you have exactly the same chance of losing 4 points whichever way you go. Thus you should take the chance of winning 2 points.

You can also think of it in the following way. Just as offering doubles is a way of maximising your gains in the games you are winning, *accepting* doubles is a way of limiting your losses in the games you are losing (as long as you still have a more than 25% chance of winning). Also remember that whenever you accept the doubling cube, you have the advantage of having exclusive use of the cube from that point on. If things *do* turn around, you (and only you) can double the stakes once again.

Let's look at how this 25% rule works in the simplest scenario. In the example on the right, it is Black's turn and he offers you a double. Should you take it?

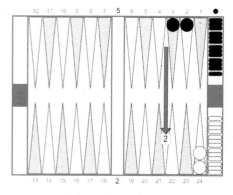

With a 31% chance of winning,
you should accept the double.

Obviously, Black has an excellent chance of winning with the next throw. But if he throws any dice combination that includes a 1 (except for a double 1), he can't win. Then you are guaranteed to win on your next turn.

So what are the chances of Black winning? There are 12 out of 36 possible throws (anything with a 1 including a double 1) that will lead to Black being unable to win on his next throw. 12 out of 36 is about 33%; thus there is a 33% chance he will not win. That is well over the 25% threshold, so you should chance the odds and take the double.

Now let's look at a slightly different position and consider what you should do if offered the double.

In the example on the right, the only throws that will prevent Black from winning are 1+1, 2+1, 1+2, 3+1, 1+3, 3+2 and 2+3. There are only 7 throws that would *not* enable Black to win. 7 out of 36 is around 19%, which is lower than your 25% threshold. In this scenario you should cut your losses and decline the double, letting Black win.

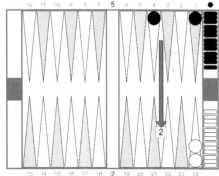

In this position there are only 7 rolls that will prevent Black from winning, so you only have around a 19% chance of winning. You should decline the double.

You can see how important it is to try to work out the statistics because, on face value, you might have thought that the first scenario gave you a lower chance of winning than the second, simply because Black seemed closer to home. Always try to work out the actual probability of winning at any stage, rather than relying on sight of the board alone.

WHEN SHOULD YOU OFFER A DOUBLE?

The thought process behind offering a double is similar to that behind accepting a double. But because the ball is in your court with the offering of doubles, you need to consider it on every move. Remember, **every roll is a new potential doubling opportunity**. The worst mistake many players make is to miss great opportunities to offer a double because they are not thinking about it before every throw. Missing an opportunity to double can cost a player the whole match.

It's vital that you offer a double before you 'lose your market', i.e. before you are so likely to win that your opponent automatically refuses. The trick is to offer a double in that window where he can be lured into accepting because he thinks he still has a chance.

Remember, if you offer a double that is accepted and you then go on to win a gammon, you win four points rather than two, so it is well worth getting it right!

Timing is *everything* when it comes to offering the doubling cube. Offer it too soon and it's a powerful tool (and potential gift) for your opponent; offer it too late and end your chances of winning both a doubled game *and* a gammon because your opponent will likely decline, forfeiting the game for only one point.

As Philip Martyn famously (to us backgammon nerds, that is) said, 'You are very easy to play against if you double either too early or too late. You may be moving your men well, but you will find yourself losing money.' And, according to Chris Bray, 'The fat lady is already singing before many doubles are offered.' If you miss that crucial moment when you can offer a double, the point at which your opponent might accept it, on the next turn it will be likely be too late. You will be too far ahead and if your opponent is a strong player, he will know not to accept the double.

Before every turn, ask yourself the following two questions in order to determine whether you should offer a double. 1) Are you winning by enough? If your chances aren't exactly 75%, are they at least close? And 2) Is there a chance that you will throw something so good that it will be too late to double on your next turn (because your opponent is sure to decline)?

If you're a beginner, you probably couldn't answer those questions without a great deal of laborious calculation, but as you play more and study the game, you will get a better feel for where you stand. Understanding your chances of winning from a particular position is something you can only learn through study and experience; it takes time.

Backgammon expert Neil Kazaross says, 'You cannot be a top tournament backgammon player if you do not know what the match equity is, believe me.'

Let's look at a couple of scenarios where you have the opportunity to offer a double.

In the scenario on the right, you clearly have a chance of winning on this turn as long as you get a double (other than double 1) or

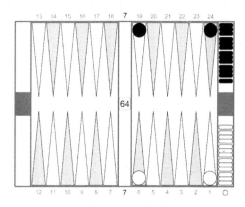

To double or not to double?

you throw a 6 with one of your dice. There are 11 ways to throw a 6. And there are 5 doubles that will allow you to finish. So that's 16 out of 36 throws will give you a win, which is around 44%. If you *don't* win, Black has the same odds with his throw, so Black has a 44% times 44% chance of winning. Black thus has a 19% chance of winning at this stage in the game. If he *doesn't* win on his next throw (after you fail to win), you will almost certainly win on your next throw (unless you are unlucky enough to throw a 2+1 twice). Thus your overall chance of winning from this position is almost 81% and Black's is a little over 19%. When you ask yourself the question do you have a 75% chance of winning, the answer is *yes*, you do!

Now let's look at the second question. If you wait one more throw, will you lose your market? Well, if you don't win on this throw and Black doesn't win on his, there is no way he would *then* accept a double on your third throw after this stage, because your chances of winning would have increased considerably, giving him much less than a 25% chance of winning.

So when you ask yourself the question: might I throw something so good that it will be too late to double on my next turn? The answer is also *yes*.

In summary, now *is* the right time to offer a double.

I assume that by now you are beginning to understand why so many of the top players are outstanding mathematicians.

In more complicated race positions the British player and writer Chris Bray suggests a simple formula for working out whether you should

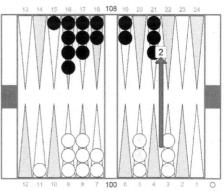

You have 100 pips to go, and it is your throw. Black has 108. You have an 8% lead so you should offer a double, which Black is likely to accept because he is behind by less than 12%.

offer a double. If you are 8% to 12% ahead on the pip count, that equates to approximately a 75% chance of winning. Thus it is time to offer or accept a double. Conversely, it's a very good rule of thumb that if you are no more than 12% behind and you are offered a double, you should take it.

THE VALUE OF HOLDING THE LIVE CUBE

As long as the game is still in play, the cube is 'live'. The person holding the **live cube** can use it again to **recube**. If your opponent offers you a double, you also want to factor in the value of possessing that live cube. You are then the only player who can offer the cube. You could use it to close out the game early or to double your potential points haul if your luck improves and you turn the game around. Kit Woolsey says, 'In general, when the decision is otherwise very close, you should lean towards a race when you own the cube, but lean towards contact positions when your opponent owns the cube.'

BASIC DOUBLING OPPORTUNITIES

There are three main scenarios where you should definitely offer or accept a double. Each takes into account your equity in the game and the timing of when you would lose your market.

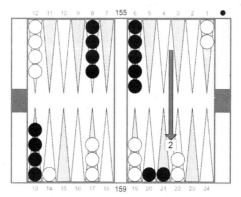

Here it is Black's throw. The players are very much still in contact and the pip count is close.

1) When you have an advantage but are still in contact (i.e. you and your opponent have not passed each other completely).

Although the pip count is close in the example shown above, you are stuck at the back and Black has a good chance of freeing one or both of his backmarkers, and even of hitting you, which would lead you to have three checkers in his home board when you re-enter. If Black threw something really good on this turn, he could lose his market. So

Black's best option is to offer the double now. You still have a more than 25% chance of winning, and because it's early in the game there are many possible scenarios for Black to get into trouble, so you should accept the double.

On the right, you are in a strong position in the race and it is your throw; there really is little chance of you not getting past Black, so if you offer the double, Black would be best advised to decline. Whenever you are offered a double, always look at the position and ask yourself, 'What's in it for me? Do I have a good play here?'

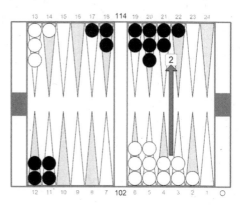

If you offer the double, Black should decline.

2) When you are past each other and racing to finish.
In the game below, the outcome isn't certain, but you are in the lead by 6 pips and it's your throw. Remember that the value of a pair of dice is on average around 8.2, so if you add that to your lead of 6 in total that's a lead of approximately 14 pips.

If you don't offer the double now and then throw something good, Black will not accept your double on your next turn and you'll miss the chance of 2 points. So you must offer now or you'll lose your market. This is probably the latest stage in this particular game where you are likely to tempt Black into accepting your double. So this kind of position, a 10% lead plus your throw, is roughly where you are likely to tempt Black into accepting,

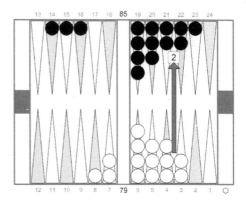

Double before you lose your market.

and then you've a good chance of winning 2 points.

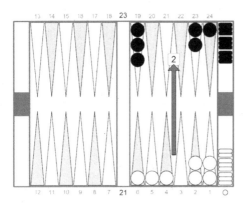

Your odds of winning are always better if you offer the double when you have around an 80% chance of winning.

3) When you want to guarantee your win.

In the scenario on the left, you can use the cube to avoid bad luck. Without the cube you would have to play the game to the bitter end. Let's go back to statistics (for those of you who can stomach it!) If you have an 80% chance of winning, this means that if you were to play five identical games up to this stage, going forward you would lose 1 in 5. Say you offered a double in each of those games (at this stage). Because your opponent only has a 20% chance of winning, he should refuse every time, i.e. in 5 out of 5 of the games. Thus, offering the doubling cube increases your odds of winning to 100%. Statistically, whenever you are at the point of having an 80% chance of winning, you should offer the double to guarantee your win. Even if Black accepts, you still have that 80% chance of winning, only this time with double the points.

At a high level, very few games are played to the end.

In the example below, the game has been pretty close but you have recently thrown a good double and have found yourself a couple of pips ahead. But it is your turn, which is an advantage at this late stage. In fact, in this scenario, Black's best option would be to decline and forfeit the game, but he may not choose to do so as it's a close call.

A MORE COMPLEX DOUBLING OPPORTUNITY

The example to the left shows a more involved situation. You have a huge lead on pips and you will likely be considering making your 5-point by moving your backmarker

What should you do with your 6+2 and when should you offer the double?

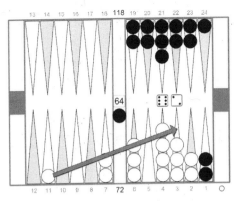

and one from your bar-point. Black's chances of re-entering on his next throw *and* hitting you (for which he'd have to throw a 6+1) would be 17 to 1. So what should you do with your 6+2 throw and when should you offer the double?

Your goal here is to try to make this your last move of the game. Instead of making your 5-point, if you can play so that Black has a zero chance of hitting you (by moving your backmarker all the way in to your 3-point, as shown above) and then you offer him a double before your next throw, he will likely decline and you'll win the game.

With your 6+2, move so that Black has no chance of hitting you and then offer the double on your next turn, which he will likely decline.

It's impossible to learn all the potential positions you could find yourself in with the cube. At the end of the day it mostly boils down to experience and study. Get some help from books, articles and mentors to help you learn. The more you play and study doubling situations, the better you will become.

And remember, both your offering decisions and your accepting decisions must be correct. Even if both your checker play and your decision-making over *accepting* double offers are better than a world champion's, if you regularly *offer* doubles at the wrong time (too early and/or too late), you will lose more often than not.

If only the backgammon books on doubling were nearly as exciting!

USING THE SCORE TO DETERMINE WHETHER OR NOT TO ACCEPT OR OFFER A DOUBLE

Before each doubling decision, you should also think about the overall score in terms of the whole match. The example below shows how your decision on whether or not to accept or offer a double changes depending on the overall match score.

The diagram below shows that you are clearly winning the race but you have one man dancing on the bar. To re-enter you need to throw a 6; you have 11 chances out of 36 of doing this. Plus you have the chance to hit Black immediately if you throw a 6+2, or hit him twice should you be lucky enough to throw a 6+6, or you could even hit him on your way around with the next throw. Given all these chances to hit Black you actually have a 30% chance of winning this game.

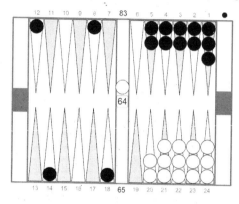

Consider the overall match score when making your doubling decisions.

If the score is 0-0, and this is the first game in a match to 5 points, Black would be wise to double at this stage. Your chances are around 30% so you should accept the offer.

Let's now imagine that Black is winning in the match by **3-2**. How would this situation change things? Black clearly has more to lose from losing 2 points because you would leapfrog into the position of leading 4-3. The next game would be a Crawford game (this is a rule that states that the doubling cube cannot be used in what is potentially the final game and we will be discussing this in more detail later), and this would give you a big advantage (because Black cannot win 2 points to leapfrog you and beat you.) If Black was leading 3-2 in the match score, he should not offer the double in this scenario.

Now, what if the score was **3-3**? Well, if Black offers you the double and you accept, he only has to win this game (which he is clearly leading) and he has won the match. So even though Black is likely to offer the double at this stage and, unless you are feeling lucky, you should decline, personally I would be tempted to accept and take my chances in this one game (because conversely if you win this game, you have won the whole match) rather than try to win two more games. Ultimately, it's a close call and somewhat depends on who you are playing.

Of course in money games there is no upper limit, you just play games for whatever the stakes are until someone folds, so the score doesn't really affect your doubling decisions.

IN YOUR OPPONENT'S SHOES

To work out if your timing is right, you may find it useful to put yourself in your opponent's shoes. How would you react to the offering of a double if you were in your opponent's position? If you're indecisive, if you think you'd be on the cusp of accepting or not accepting, then this is the perfect time to double. If means you've got the timing just right. If, from your opponent's perspective you'd *definitely* take your double, you've offered too soon. If you'd definitely *decline* the offer, you've offered too late.

In their book, Oswald Jacoby and John Crawford say, 'In all gambling games there is a loser's syndrome which keeps people continuing on when they're behind and going further into the hole. The doubling feature in backgammon makes this syndrome far more dangerous.'

Remember, doubling too early is one of the worst mistakes you can make in backgammon. If the game turns against you (as can often happen), your opponent has all the power because he controls the cube and can thus double you back at his whim, making it a 4-point match. If you lose a gammon as well, that's 8 points against you. When you offer the cube too early, it is usually an easy decision for your opponent to accept it.

THE GAMMON EFFECT

A player's chance of winning a gammon changes the match equity position and is affected by the overall match score, so you should always be aware of your chances, and your opponent's chances, of winning a gammon. If, for example, you accept a double when you are only two points away from winning the match, the value of a winning a gammon to you becomes zero; you don't *need* to win a gammon to win the match because you will be getting 2 points (and thus winning the match) if you win this game. Equally, there is no value in you holding the cube at this point because you don't need the points to win.

But say you are on 3-1 in a game to 5 points. Although you only need 2 points to win the match, your opponent can win the match with 4 points. If your opponent offers you the cube and you accept, but then he goes on to win a gammon, you will lose the entire match. The price of losing a gammon in this scenario is very high. In fact, in this situation, the value of a gammon (to your opponent) is equal to the value of winning a game. If you win the game you win the match; if you lose a gammon you lose the match. At this score, 3-1, you have to be much more careful about accepting a cube if you are at risk of losing a gammon.

It may seem a daunting task to try to estimate your odds of winning and losing a gammon, but with some practice and the help of a computer programme (that will automatically tell you your odds until you get used to recognizing certain patterns), you'll soon get the hang of it. There are some obvious general patterns. If you have more backmarkers, you get gammoned more; if you have an anchor, you get gammoned less. If you have a high anchor, you get gammoned even less. Skilled players can often do these estimates within a percentage point or two for most positions.

In the example on the right, you have a clear lead. But you also have a good chance of getting a gammon because Black has three backmarkers in your home board.

Even though Black still has around a 30% chance of winning, now is a good time for you to offer the double before it's too late (because Black will soon be too worried about losing a gammon to accept).

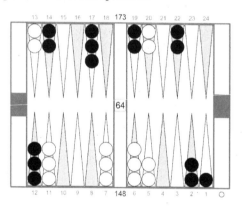

You have a good chance of getting a gammon.

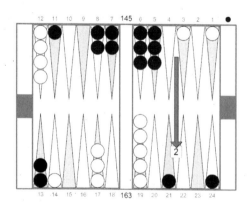

Without a prime made, you should not accept the double.

PRIME VERSUS PRIME

You can make a quick decision about accepting a double if you are playing 'prime against prime'. If you are offered a double and your opponent has a strong prime, you should only accept if you have an equally strong prime. In the example on the left, Black is correct to offer you a double. However, you haven't made a prime yet, so your position is too weak to accept.

A FREE DROP

After a Crawford game (where no doubles are allowed), if the match hasn't ended, at least one player remains within one point of winning. In this scenario, for the losing player there is no downside to offering a double as soon as possible. In fact, it's silly not to turn the cube to 2 when your opponent only needs 1 point because this is the only way you can leapfrog him.

But is it correct always to accept this double at the start of the game? Not if your opponent needs an even number of points to win.

If the match is to seven points and you are winning 6-5, then the match will be decided either on this game if you accept the double or on the next game if you refuse it. If your opponent has a slight lead (for example, he has started with an excellent throw like a 3+1) then at this point he has more than a 50% chance of winning this game and the match (if you accept the double and continue playing). In this scenario, you would be better off refusing a double, dropping the game, letting the score go to 6-6 and taking your chances in the next game where no one will need to offer the doubling cube anyway. This is called a '**free drop**'.

But say the score was 6-4 in a match to seven points. Now you must accept the double, even if your opponent is leading in the current game. He would still have to win two games (unless he wins a gammon, in which case it's all over for you). If you drop this game, on the next game your opponent offers you the double on his first roll and only needs to win one game to win the match.

Many people get confused and either don't use their free drop when they should or drop when they think they have a free drop and don't. Making either of these mistakes will cost you winning chances, so really familiarize yourself with this tactic.

DOUBLING RIGHT BACK ('THE BEAVER')

If you are offered a double that you are very happy to accept because you feel your chances of winning are particularly high, you can actually double again immediately and still retain control of the cube. When you accept the double, you say, 'I beaver,' and turn the cube over again. You would only do this if your opponent has made a huge mistake (from his standpoint in the game) in offering you the double and you are absolutely sure that the odds are very much in your favour.

This is a highly unusual move and most tournaments don't allow beavers. The tactic is usually only used in matches for money.

MORE ABOUT MATCH SCORES

For real statistics nerds, let's go even further into the percentages here. We call the point at which you should accept a doubles offer the 'take point'. As we've shown, a 25% chance of winning is only the take point when the score in terms of games is completely even (or only one game is being played). Let's see how this is affected, statistically, depending on what the match equity is.

It's always useful to think in terms of a match to 5 points because you can use the knowledge to help you in the last 5 points of any match. For example, if you are playing to 35 points, at the start of the match you are both so far from the finishing line that your chances are similar, but as you get closer to the end, you might end up 5 points apart. At this stage, it becomes exactly like a match to 5 points.

	% chance of winning	take point for leader
4 / 5 (1-0)	58%	19%
3 / 5 (2-0)	67%	18%
2 / 5 (3-0)	75%	17%
1 / 5 (4-0)	84%	Crawford game, no doubles
3 / 4 (2-1)	57%	21%
2 / 4 (3-1)	67%	20%
1 / 4 (4-1)	81%	Crawford game, no doubles
2 / 3 (3-2)	60%	26%
1 / 3 (4-2)	75%	Crawford game, no doubles
1 / 2 (4-3)	68%	Crawford game, no doubles

Match equity is always best defined by looking at the number of points away from victory you are, rather than looking at the score. If you are 2 points ahead at the start of a match but you need 17 points to win, the advantage is fairly meaningless, but if you are 2 points ahead and you only need 3 to win the match, this is significant.

If you are in a 5-point match and you are leading 1-0, your chances of winning the match are 58%. Thus your opponent's chances are 42%. If you are level (whether you are at 0-0 or 4-4), your chances are 50% each.

The table below shows how many points away from winning you are in a 5-point match (i.e. the number of points you need to finish the match). This is the score that really matters. So if the score is 3-1 in a five-point match, the leader is 2 points away from winning and the player who is behind (or 'trailing') is 4 points away. The table shows the 'take points' for the leader (i.e. the percentage chance he should have of winning in order to offer or accept the doubling cube).

The numbers on the left show how many points you are away from victory and how many points away your opponent is (the actual score being shown in brackets).

Now you can see how your doubling point and take point vary depending on your match equity (i.e. your percentage chance of winning). For example, if you are winning 3-1, it's more in your opponent's interest to double than yours, because you are the strong favourite to win without needing to double, whereas your opponent can leapfrog you with doubles.

Doubling is a complex subject and a lot to take in all at once. Don't worry; as you practice these principles will slowly become familiar.

© PinkFloydFanPage

Pink Floyd's Dave Gilmour and Roger Waters in the good old days...

13

BRINGING OUT YOUR BACK GAME

Never, ever, grab the first good-looking play you see. There is often a better move around the corner. Go look for it.

KIT WOOLSEY

During a stint living in New York in the 1990s, I went to watch the New York Knicks play the Chicago Bulls and was lucky enough to see Michael Jordan play. At one point in the game, he made a bad mistake, causing him to lose the ball before he could shoot. Furiously, he ran back the length of the court, threw himself at the defender, regained the ball and then ran all the way back up the court to score.

That is the basketball version of playing a great back game. It was a great recovery. Of course, Jordan would have preferred not to lose the ball in the first place and you should aim not to have to recover from your mistakes, but if you do find yourself 'losing the ball', there is nothing so satisfying as playing a really good back game and coming back to win.

A **back game** is the strategy you use to recover a game you're losing, to try to get a shot at winning again. It becomes necessary after you've been hit several times and have started losing in the race, but when you've managed to make two or more anchors in your opponent's home board. These will help you fight back. You really need two anchors to make it a back game. If you only have one anchor it's a **holding game** but in my experience you're unlikely to win from this position.

You often hear beginners talking about bringing out their back game. Once they start losing and find themselves stuck at the back they say, 'Okay it's time to bring out my back game'. That doesn't mean they know what to do, it just means they know they're losing!

There is nothing more fun and satisfying than, when it looked like you were being slaughtered, your back game turns things around and you get a shot – often two – at hitting your opponent. Many players intentionally hold back to play a back game because they love this gambit so much. What they forget is that there is still a very real chance that they won't get the opportunity to hit, so it's a risky tactic.

The back game recovery is not a position you should try to put yourself in, even though it looks great when you can pull it off. You should always prioritise winning in the normal course of play rather than letting yourself get into a risky, heart-stopping situation. Remember if your back game fails, you will often lose a gammon (twice the points the game was worth) and sometimes even a backgammon (triple the points the game was worth).

If you have one man trapped at the back you will feel as helpless as Paul Sheldon (the author who is captured and tied down by a psychotic fan in Stephen King's *Misery*). But having a whole team trapped in your opponent's home board is far more hopeful, more like *Escape to Victory*.

The key to playing a good back game, having established a couple of points deep in your opponent's home board, is to build a very strong home board yourself so that when you do get that essential opportunity to hit, it really counts. However, timing is everything. It won't work if you don't get the timing right. If you are forced to destroy your home board with throws that you don't want while your two anchors are trapped in your opponent's home board, then hitting your opponent will be a hollow victory because he will be he will be able to re-enter easily and make a recovery.

You can play a back game (as opposed to a holding game) when you have two anchors in your opponent's home board, for example when you're holding his 1-point and 3-point as shown to the right.

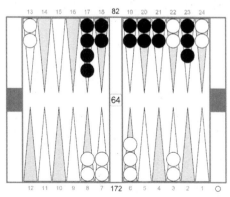

You have a 1-point and 3-point back game.

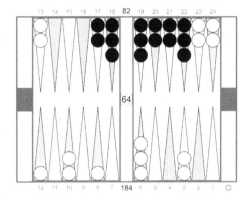

When you have a 1-point and 2-point back game.

The 1-point and 2-point back game, as shown on the left, can also be effective, but because you are so far back, by the time you get the opportunity to hit, it might be too late to escape.

It is also effective to play a back game from further along the opponent's home board if his prime is further back, like this... Black is still the favourite to win here, however.

The modern-day experts are not even calling games that look like this final example 'back games' anymore, but rather '**double-holding games**', because you really aren't far enough *back*. By definition, a back game means that you are

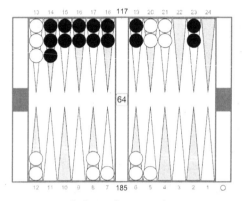

A back game that is not so deep.

holding a couple of points right at the back of your opponent's board and not too far along. You can see why it is such a risky strategy. If you don't get some good opportunities to hit, you can pretty much kiss this game goodbye. The only advantage to a double-holding game over a true back game is that, because you are further forward, you do slightly lower your risk of losing a gammon or backgammon because you've got a better chance of making it home and bearing off at least one checker before your opponent finishes bearing off his checkers.

Also remember that there is generally no need to keep more than two checkers on a point, especially when you are simply holding anchors and there are no more builders needed. So if you have more than two checkers on one point, try to run the extra ones around the board when you can; or you could use them to try to block your opponent even further by building more points on his side of the board.

'The secret of good comedy...' as Rowan Atkinson and Richard Curtis have told us, '...is timing'. The same goes for a back game. At first it feels counterintuitive, but you will need ample time to hit your opponent. If you already have a perfect home board by the time you hit, you will have advanced too far. You will have (as players often say) 'crashed'. Crashing is when you are forced to move your checkers deeper and deeper into your home board, which leave free points for your opponent to land on when you hit him... defeating the object of the back game. Crashing is a frustrating experience when you've put a lot of hard work into building a strong home board.

In the example on the right, you still have a decent chance of winning (specifically a 30% chance) but you must make sure that, if you do hit your opponent, your home board is as primed as possible. Plus, you want to avoid a gammon, so you move a checker rather than crashing your home board. The blot you leave behind can still be dangerous to your opponent.

Keep a checker, run a checker... but save your home board.

It can also be powerful to have a 2-point-prime in your opponent's board. In the position below, your throw of 2+2 can create a double anchor, which will give you the best chance of blocking your opponent. Your timing is good here because you have plenty of time to move around the board with your midmarkers and build your home board while you wait for opportunities to hit your opponent.

When your anchors are several spaces apart, rather than being side-by-side in a prime, we call it a **split back game**. In this situation, it is easier for your opponent to bring his checkers home, so you should avoid getting into this position if possible. Again, never hold out for

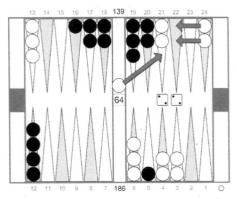

Creating a 4-point and 3-point back game.

a back game anyway; a back game should be avoided at all costs. If you are presented with a chance to **play forward** and change your game plan to a running or priming game, you should always take it. But if you find yourself in a back game and don't get the opportunity to play forward, then commit to it fully, don't be timid and half-hearted about it. Too many players become afraid of getting gammoned and start playing cautiously when in a back game. Ironically, this is more likely to lead to you getting gammoned than if you play boldly!

A 3-POINT-PRIME BACK GAME

Holding a 3-point-prime in your opponent's home board is often a winning strategy... as long as time is on your side.

Below, you have a 60% chance of winning from this position. Often your opponent has made the huge mistake of giving you the cube simply on the basis of his large numerical lead.

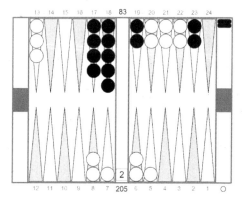

A 3-point-prime in your opponent's board
gives you a strong back game.

Make sure your home checkers are not too far advanced though; otherwise your chances diminish because your board is going to crash. By the time you get the opportunities you need to hit, you are likely to have a home board with checkers stacked so close to home that you will not be able to contain your opponent.

BUILDING TOWARDS A BACK GAME

So how do you build towards a back game, if you begin to realize you might need one?

On the right we can see how you could use your throw of 4+3 to make two home board points, but the better choice is to expose one of your midmarkers instead. Even though you put yourself at risk of being hit, this doesn't outweigh the benefit of the move. In fact, being hit at this point could help the timing of your back game because it buys you more time, saving you from crashing your home board.

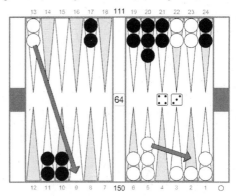

Expose one of your midmarkers to save your home board from crashing subsequently.

WHEN TO CUT AND RUN

Exactly how long should you hang on for before deciding to cut and run? This is often a difficult decision. If you are playing a back game but have failed to hit, when should you cut and run to save being gammoned? Of course, it depends on the score but it is generally best to hang around for as long as you believe you are still in with a chance of hitting. At the same time, you must try to work out at what stage you need to run to avoid being gammoned. A very important consideration here, whether you are at a score where a gammon will hurt you considerably (even cost you the match) or at a score where the effect of a gammon will be almost negligible.

Hollywood greats Cary Grant and Randolph Scott, 1932.

14

NUMBER
CRUNCHING

*Do not worry about your difficulties
in mathematics.
I can assure you mine are still greater.*

ALBERT EINSTEIN

A lot of backgammon is about counting. If you get your head around the numbers, you will steadily improve. I wasn't thinking about the numbers and didn't know I needed to when I had some early success in reaching the final of a tournament at White's in London. This was the first time I met and spoke with Phil Simborg, a world-class professional teacher and player from Chicago. Phil is funny and kind, but he always 'tells it like it is' . We played a game or two and he said, 'Simon, I wanted to play a game with you to determine whether you were lucky to get as far as you did at the White's tournament or if you're a really strong player. Let me tell you, you've been lucky... you need to work at this!'

I gleaned many pearls of wisdom from Phil. He advised me to play more tournaments and online matches, to play against a good computer programme, and to read some books about the game.

To get more live practice I entered the London Open. I was asked whether I wanted to join the professional or the amateur draw. Technically I was an amateur, but I couldn't resist the opportunity to go up against professionals and the subsequent right to brag about it unreservedly if I did well, so I decided to enter both. I perversely relished the possibility of being knocked out twice in a day.

The London Open... lots of bean counters.

As I entered Brown's Hotel, there was an apprehensive atmosphere and plenty of adrenaline-fuelled good humour. Backgammon players are a friendly crowd even when the stakes are high and this tournament was no exception. I was struck by how academic and studious some of the players seemed; we could have been in a university maths department common room. Indeed, it turned out that many of the players were highly skilled at maths. Chartered accountants and taxi drivers alike were rapidly crunching numbers, calculating the odds.

In the professional draw, a couple of players wore headphones throughout their match. I assumed they were listening to music, but a fellow competitor explained to me that they were merely blocking out the noise of their opponents. I was struck by how focused they were, they weren't there to make friends or have a chat (which, for me, is often half the point of a good backgammon match), and they certainly weren't there to have fun, although many other players clearly were.

One competitor in the amateur draw told me about her successful book, which outlined a new technique for coaching maths to children. I didn't understand her explanation of it even after she repeated it, so I told her I hoped I wasn't playing one of her young pupils in the first round.

It wasn't my day in the end; I lost early on in the amateur contest. In the professional draw, I was pleased that I managed to beat an accountant in the first round, but then I was knocked out in the second round by an economic forecaster. That day I learnt that, while I'll never be a walking calculator like some of those brilliant players, learning to think about the numbers in the right way will help anyone to become a winner at backgammon.

PIPS... 167 AND COUNTING

Having a good idea of who is ahead in the **pip count** — which measures the number of moves each player is away from bearing all their counters off the board — and by how much, will help you make better decisions.

Have a look at the board's starting position. At the start of the game, the pip count is **167 pips** for both players.

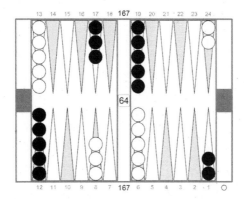

Each player is 167 pips away from finishing.

Here's how the pips work at the start of the game. If your opponent offered no resistance and you were never hit or blocked, you would need 167 pips to move all the checkers around and off the board.

We can count these 167 moves as follows.

Your two backmarkers are on your 24-point, so that's **48 pips** needed to bear them off the board. Your five midmarkers are each 13 pips away from being borne off, so that's 5x13, or another **65 pips**. Next are the three checkers on your 8-point; they will take 8 pips each to bear off, making another **24 pips**. And finally the 5 checkers on your 6-point in your home board need 6 moves each to be borne off, so that's 5x6, in other words **30 pips**. The grand total is 48+65+24+30, which comes to **167 pips**.

When you play backgammon against a computer program or online, you can adjust your settings to show the pip count. This is extremely useful because it tells you, at any point in the game, who is ahead in the race to finish, and by how many pips. If you're playing on a conventional board you should learn to keep a mental estimate of approximately how many pips you have left.

In a live match you won't have time to count the exact pips but it's important to develop a feeling for how much you are winning or losing by. There are many complicated ways to do this, but the simplest is called a **cancellation count**, in which you don't bother to calculate the total pip count but merely estimate one side's lead. To do this, quickly compare the positions of your checkers with the positions of your opponent's. Cancel out any checkers in the same position. Just count the ones in different positions and compare them. That should show you if, for example, you are ahead by 9 pips or your opponent has a lead of 12 pips, etc. You don't have the time to count the exact pips before every move, and using your knowledge of the pip count is not an exact science anyway. However, after you've done it many times you should be able to get a feel for who is leading in the pip race fairly quickly. Knowing who is ahead is the vital information that you need; don't worry too much about the overall totals.

The more you play, the easier you'll find it to calculate the pip totals for you and your opponent simply by glancing at the board. This will also help you get a feel for how far advanced the game is. If you spend all your time playing against a computer, which calculates and displays the pip count for you, you won't learn to count the pips for yourself and you'll be at a disadvantage when you play a real person on a conventional board. So get out there and play some real games once in a while!

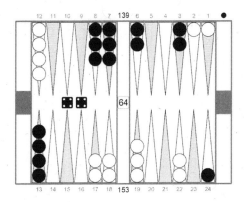

Can you make a quick calculation of who has more pips to go?

At first glance, this board seems to show a position where both players are on almost equal pips. However, if you look a little closer you'll see that Black has a pip count of 139, while White has 153 pips to go, so Black has a pip count lead of 14 over you. Additionally, Black has thrown a 4+4 which gives him another 16 pips and he isn't blocked so he can legitimately move all of his 4-moves. At the end of his throw he will be 30 pips ahead, at 123 against your 153. That's a big lead, big enough to change the way you should now think of how to approach this game strategically.

Becoming familiar with the pip count and knowing, at all times, whether you are up or down in the race will help you make better decisions. Sometimes you will be so far behind in the race to finish that your best chance of winning is to slow the race down by trying to delay your opponent. Knowing the approximate pip count will also help you make better decisions about doubling. You should always consider the pip count, no matter what stage you are at. Even the most experienced players sometimes forget (or don't know) that there is no position in backgammon where the pip count isn't a factor.

Again, this is why mathematicians excel at backgammon. Art Benjamin is a Math Professor at Harvey Mudd College. He is the author of several books on mathematics and has appeared on many television shows, entertaining audiences all over the world with his MathMagic show (he calls himself a mathemagician!) One year he decided to play in a lot of backgammon tournaments and ended up No. 1 on the U.S. tour!

The **average value of a throw** from two dice is 8.2, which is probably higher than you might have assumed. This is

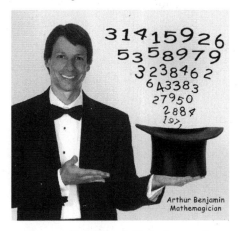

Maths whizz, Art Benjamin

because doubles (where you get to make each move of the dice twice) push up the average. Remembering this can help you assess the game, especially in a race.

If you have an average of 8.2 moves on each throw, you need (on average) about 20 throws to make up your 167 pips to finish. Of course, a game is highly unlikely to go so smoothly that you are never hit (which means clocking up more pips), or blocked from moving, but it's still useful information.

Many players drift through their matches without stopping to think because they assume that the direct route to getting round (i.e. in around 20 moves) is quite likely; but this isn't the case. Players with this mindset try to make every move as safely as possible, avoiding leaving blots and taking risks, only to discover that this 'safe' strategy carries more risk than they'd bargained for. If they've safely stacked up their checkers on only a few points and haven't made a number of good, strategic points to act as 'stepping stones' when they do need to move, they'll find they become vulnerable at a more critical stage later on in the game. If your strategy is always just to race to the end of the game faster than your opponent, backgammon will quickly become very frustrating because an opponent who has put a little more thought into their game can ruin your plans pretty much every time.

WHY THINKING ABOUT YOUR MOVES MATTERS

The actual number of possible moves in a backgammon game is rather mind-boggling. Let's say you move first, then your opponent has his turn and then you move again. There are 21 different outcomes to any throw of the dice, so in just the first three moves of a game, there are 9,261 (21x21x21) different combinations. There are often more than 50 moves in a single game so the number of different combinations becomes astronomical (50^{20}) and even increases as the number goes up, due to players getting hit and blocked. Remember this number is only showing how many different combinations of throws there are in a game. Add to that your *choices* of moves with each throw of the dice and the number becomes almost unimaginable. Champion player and author, Walter Trice, estimated that there are **over a trillion** possible legal positions that can be attained on a backgammon board!

So it won't work just to memorise some of these trillion moves. It's much better to understand why a certain move is good and apply that thinking in different situations. Even if you learn the opening moves by heart, you still need to think the moves through every time and understand why you are making each choice.

With a better understanding of the game, you'll be surprised how quickly assessing your next move becomes second nature to you. In life, sometimes we need to ignore the huge possibilities that lie before us and just live in the present, focusing on what we need to achieve in the immediate future. The same applies in backgammon. For the most part, you should just focus on your best move in the moment.

When you are using two dice, although there are **36 (6x6) possible dice throws**, there are only **21 different outcomes** because there are two different ways of throwing all the numbers except for doubles. For example, 3+4 counts as a different roll to 4+3. Because the different numbers could come up on either of the two dice, you are twice as likely to throw a combination of 4 and 3 than to throw a 4+4. Some people find this difficult to grasp at first.

I have listed **all 36 possible throws** below to help you estimate the odds of what you or your opponent might throw next.

	Dice 1		Dice 2	Total pips visible on both dice (not doubles)
1.	1	and	1	2
2.	1	and	2	3
3.	2	and	1	3
4.	2	and	2	4
5.	3	and	1	4
6.	1	and	3	4
7.	3	and	2	5
8.	2	and	3	5
9.	4	and	1	5
10.	1	and	4	5
11.	3	and	3	6
12.	4	and	2	6
13.	2	and	4	6
14.	5	and	1	6
15.	1	and	5	6
16.	4	and	3	7
17.	3	and	4	7
18.	5	and	2	7
19.	2	and	5	7
20.	6	and	1	7
21.	1	and	6	7
22.	4	and	4	8
23.	5	and	3	8
24.	3	and	5	8
25.	6	and	2	8
26.	2	and	6	8
27.	6	and	3	9
28.	3	and	6	9
29.	5	and	4	9
30.	4	and	5	9
31.	5	and	5	10
32.	6	and	4	10
33.	4	and	6	10
34.	6	and	5	11
35.	5	and	6	11
36.	6	and	6	12

HITTING A NUMBER WITH ONE DICE

Now we're familiar with the 36 different throws of the dice and the 21 different outcomes, let's take a look at how likely you are to throw each number. This is going to come in handy because you'll need to have a good idea of what chances you or your opponent have of throwing a particular number in many situations.

Let's take the example that your opponent has two blots and you need either a total of 6 or a total of 10 to hit one of them, and to keep it simple let's assume there is nothing blocking your way from either blot. You're more likely to throw a total number between 1 and 6 than between 7 and 12 because it can be achieved with either one dice or two. Throwing a 10 can *only* be achieved with using the combination of moves on two dice, but throwing a 6 can be achieved with one dice *or* with a combination of two dice. You therefore have a lot more chances of throwing a 6.

A good statistic to remember from the table of throws above is the number of chances of any particular number (not a combination) from 1 to 6 coming up with two dice. You have 11 in 36 chances of throwing any number from 1 to 6. For example, you can roll a 3 with any of the following 11 combinations: 3+1, 1+3, 3+2, 2+3, 3+3, 3+4, 4+3, 3+5, 5+3, 3+6 and 6+3. So for example if you have been hit and the only gap in your opponent's home board is point number 3, you know that you have an 11 in 36 chance (just under a 1 in 3 chance) of re-entering with your next throw.

HITTING A NUMBER WITH TWO DICE

A good rule of thumb is that if you are trying to throw a number from 1 to 6, the higher the number the more chances you have because there are more ways to do it with two dice. For example, throwing the number 1 can only be done if at least one of your dice is a 1, so this only happens 11 out of every 36 times. But throwing a total of 5 can be done using four other combinations of both dice (3+2, 2+3, 4+1 and 1+4) as well as the 11 rolls that contain a 5, so you have a total of 15 out of 36 ways you can roll a total of 5 and move 5 spaces (assuming you're not blocked from using any of the throws if you're combining the dice).

To confirm this, take a quick look at the table listing the 36 throws. You can see that, in the case of the number 1, there are 11 times this single digit comes up, from 1 +1 all the way through to 6+1.

Here is a breakdown of the odds of throwing a number below 7, including combinations:

Throwing any combination of 1 with two dice: 11 chances out of 36

Throwing any combination of 2 with two dice: 12 chances out of 36

Throwing any combination of 3 with two dice: 14 chances out of 36

Throwing any combination of 4 with two dice: 15 chances out of 36

Throwing any combination of 5 with two dice: 15 chances out of 36

Throwing any combination of 6 with two dice: 17 chances out of 36

Any old 6…. Odds of throwing a 6 with one or both dice: 17/36.

Lucky 7… Odds of throwing a 7 with one or both dice: 6/36.

There's a big difference between the two, isn't there? Without the magic of being able to throw your required number with a single dice, your chances get much smaller.

Most of us vaguely remember 7 is the most likely throw you can get in dice games such as Craps, because 7 is right in the middle of the range of numbers you could throw. But there are still only six ways to throw a 7. These are 5+2, 2+5, 4+3, 3+4, 6+1, and 1+6. That's it.

To throw a 7 or above, we fall off a precipice in terms of our chances of getting a particular number with two dice, and it's downhill from there in terms of how likely you are to throw any combination with a pair of dice. This is also very useful to know.

Here's the rest of the list, showing the **odds of throwing a number or combination of 7 and above:**

Throwing any combination of 7 with two dice: 6 chances out of 36

Throwing any combination of 8 with two dice: 6 chances out of 36

Throwing any combination of 9 with two dice: 5 chances out of 36

Throwing any combination of 10 with two dice: 3 chances out of 36

Throwing any combination of 11 with two dice: 2 chances out of 36

Throwing any combination of 12 with two dice:	3 chances out of 36
Throwing any combination of 15 with two dice:	1 chance out of 36
Throwing any combination of 16 with two dice:	1 chance out of 36
Throwing any combination of 18 with two dice:	1 chance out of 36
Throwing any combination of 20 with two dice:	1 chance out of 36
Throwing any combination of 24 with two dice:	1 chance out of 36

Remember this list includes doubles, so for example you have 3 chances of throwing a 12. You can do this with a 4+4, 3+3 or a 6+6.

There are gaps in the table because there are certain numbers which no possible combination of dice will deliver. For example, try as you might, you can never throw a 13!

You don't have to learn this table but try at least to become familiar with it. Try to become at least on nodding terms with your chances of getting a particular number. It's worth knowing, for example, that you have five times the probability of throwing a 5 than a 12. That's a big difference and might well affect your thinking when making a decision in a particular situation.

LEAVE A LONG SHOT, NOT A SHORT SHOT

Let's look at two almost identical examples that show how having an understanding of this table can really make a big difference.

In the first example, as shown below, Black has to throw a 7 in order for his backmarker to hit White's blot on his 17-point. His chances of doing so are 6 in 36.

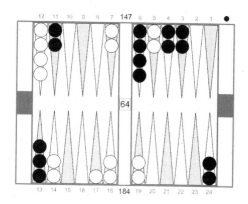

Black needs a 7 to hit; he has a 6 in 36 chance.

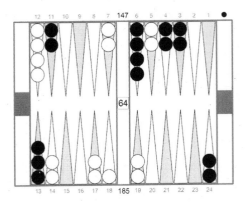

Here Black needs a 6 to hit and therefore has a much better chance (17/36).

But if your blot was just one point closer, and Black only needed to throw a 6 (as shown in the slightly different example to the left), Black's chances leap up to 17 in 36, which is a big difference. Black is almost 3 times more likely to be able to hit the White blot in this second example just because your checker is now one point nearer to his backmarkers.

When you leave a blot that could be hit by your opponent, we call it leaving a shot. Always try to leave a long shot (preferably more than 6 spaces away) rather than a short shot as you can dramatically reduce your opponent's chances of hitting it.

A FLUKE

I played in a tournament recently where at one point in the game I had a checker on the bar because I'd just been hit. I needed to throw any number *except* for a 5 or a 6 (because my opponent had created a 2-point-prime on his 5-point and 6-point) in order for my checker to re-enter the board. At my first attempt, I threw 6+6. I could not get on. On my next turn I threw a 6+5; I still couldn't re-enter. On my third attempt I was thwarted again, by throwing another 6+6. I failed *yet again* to re-enter. What are the odds of that? Well, they are a little over 20,000 to 1, so I was feeling rather hard done by!

However, later on in the same game my luck became as outrageously good as it had been bad and the game turned around in my favour. Finally I found myself needing to throw a double to win not just the game but also a rare backgammon and, sure enough, I managed to do so.

In the same game I had experienced unbelievably bad luck followed by extremely good luck. Backgammon is the only game of skill where your luck can fluctuate so dramatically. One thing I do believe (and every good player needs to believe in order not to go crazy playing this game) is that in the long run, luck evens out, and the better you play the 'luckier' you will be overall!

Bob Dylan, taking time out from the Rolling Thunder Revue tour, 1975.

15

TOP TIPS

There are three steps that should be taken
EVERY time it is your turn to play:

1. Have a plan.
2. Consider the cube.
3. Choose the best move.

Thinking about these three things,
in the above order,
should become second nature.

KENT GOULDING

I *was once invited to an evening of backgammon at the Roehampton Club in West London. Quite late in the evening, I found myself up against a player who hadn't played much backgammon but happened to be a very experienced bridge player. I was tired and hungry, having watched the buffet being devoured by other players while I was still playing my first match.*

Wanting to move quickly through the match, I offered an early, over-confident double, which was accepted. Predictably, and deservedly, my luck left the building and I found myself down 0-2 in a match to five. I was annoyed with myself for my arrogance and presumption that I could bully my inexperienced opponent. There's nothing wrong with changing your tactics against a less able player and taking advantage of your knowledge, but it's very feeble to do so recklessly and motivated by the desire to finish the game and get some dinner. The better tactical decision would have been to plod through the games without offering doubles. The chances of a novice winning a match to five played over nine games without doubles being used is much less than if only two or three games are played with points doubled using the cube. So take it slowly when playing a weaker player.

One sportsman who was brilliant at playing against weak opposition was Graeme Hick. Hick was a wonderful cricketer and one of the leading batsmen of his generation, but he was plagued throughout his career by fans and journalists calling him a 'flat track bully'. In other words, against modest opposition and on a calm batting surface he was spectacularly good. He once famously scored a quadruple century for Worcestershire against Somerset. (For those of you who don't follow cricket, this is a rare achievement that happens only once in a very long while). However, when he was playing in international cricket against the best spin bowlers on tricky batting services, Graeme consistently underperformed.

In backgammon, as you get more confident, you can become something of a flat track bully yourself. In other words, when playing against an inexperienced opponent, you can take advantage of him by offering aggressive doubles and getting away with overly confident moves. There's nothing wrong with that, but it won't stand up in a big tournament against seasoned opponents. When you meet your match, you'll quickly lose out if you don't use a smart game plan and make too many risky decisions.

Graeme Hick, making that track slightly flatter.

Play the player, but be smart about it.

I now want to share with you some of the best backgammon tips I have to offer from my years of studying and talking to top players.

TOP TIP 1: CHOOSE THE RIGHT MOVE

Malcolm Davis, winner of many tournaments says, 'Never think about winning and losing just think about the right play. You can't control the outcome but you can control what you do.'

Remember, when you think you know the right move to make, always look for a better move and then compare your options. In the position on the right, you've thrown a 2+1, the lowest possible dice combination in the game, but it is not necessarily the worst throw. In fact, you are spoilt for choice in this scenario. Clearly you could make your own 5-point. But look more

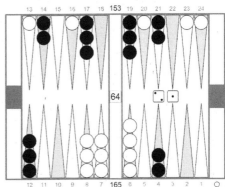

Consider all your choices.

closely. Better still, you could make your own mid-point. But wait, you could also make your opponent's 3-point.

In fact, if you do any of these things, you are making a blunder... because there is an even *better* move! That is to make your opponent's 5-point, as you've done on the right. With your opponent having moved his backmarkers, and given the number of blots you've left in his back yard, making his 5-point underpins your game.

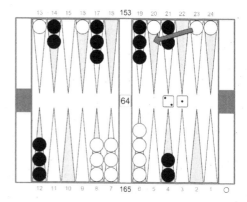

The best choice is to make your opponent's 5-point.

Remember, the best move the one is not necessarily the one you spotted first. Top players don't get excited when they first see a good move; they pause and look around to see what else is available. Then they weigh up the various choices before deciding what's best.

TOP TIP 2: OFFENCE/OFFENCE; DEFENCE/DEFENCE

Phil Simborg gave me this great tip for situations where you have a number of choices. He says that if you find yourself in an offensive position, you should always play an offensive move, and vice versa. If you find yourself in a defensive position, make a more defensive move. Looking again at the example given above in the previous tip, if you have 5 blots around the board that can be readily attacked by Black on his next roll, you need to play defensively. No matter what you do you will still have some blots, but if you make your opponent's 5-point you prevent him from either blitzing or priming you. If you had made your own 5-point, Black has multiple ways to hit you twice or make points around your blots.

'Backgammon is like war,' Phil says. 'You are fighting for territory.'

When you are outnumbered and out-gunned, you dig in and await reinforcements or for things to get better. But when you are the one on the attack and you have more troops (checkers), this is not the time to wait and give your opponent a chance to breathe. As Phil charmingly says, 'When he's having trouble breathing, step on his windpipe!'

Hindsight isn't always a wonderful thing. Often, even when you do the right thing you still get punished for it. This is true both in backgammon and in life! But this is one of the reasons people love the game; it's so unpredictable. However, if you do make a move that is correct and then doesn't work out for you, don't beat yourself up over it or waste time wishing you'd done something differently. You know that, statistically, in different circumstances that move would have paid off for you. Don't let your mind trick you into thinking otherwise. Likewise, you might sometimes make the wrong play and it works beautifully. Be honest with yourself about this and don't take away a misguided lesson.

TOP TIP 3: LEAVE A PAIR BEHIND A PRIME, NOT A BLOT

If you have to leave checkers behind a prime, it can often actually be better to have two as together they can make a powerful stand, whereas one on its own is cannon fodder.

Consider the following two examples. In the first, you have two backmarkers and in the second you only have one. When you have two you have around a 33% chance of winning, but with one backmarker you have only a 20% chance.

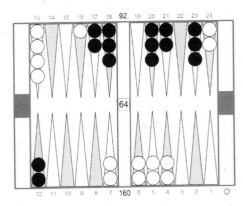

You have a pair of backmarkers left.

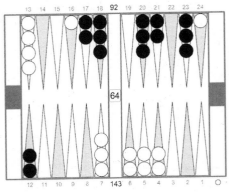

You only have one backmarker left behind.

TOP TIP 4: DO YOUR MOVES LOOK ELEGANT?

Elegant moves often tell you that you've made the right play. It might be safe to stack eight checkers on the same point when you throw a double but you might agree that this doesn't look quite right, and you should be able to see that you've created an unbalanced board. If the move wouldn't leave an elegant looking board, take a closer look and see how you might do things differently.

TOP TIP 5: DON'T ACCEPT A DOUBLE JUST TO FIND OUT WHAT HAPPENS AT THE END!

Even professionals do this sometimes and I know one former world champion who has done it regularly in recent times ('former' being the operative word!) It's easy to do. When you are playing a thrilling match, you feel the gravitational pull towards finishing it and finding out if you could actually execute your wonderful back-game strategy. If you refuse the double you will never know if you could have survived. Don't be tempted if you calculate that the odds say you shouldn't accept.

TOP TIP 6: BE AN OPTIMIST

Player and writer Walter Trice says, 'Winners are people who expect to win.' Good players are generally optimists; they always see some chance to win, even when things look very dark. And because they see the silver lining — and play for it instead of giving up, as many players would do in the same situation — they end up winning more as a result.

Chris Bray: enjoying his winnings?

TOP TIP 7: KNOWING THE THEORY ISN'T EVERYTHING

As well as playing and writing about backgammon, Chris Bray also gives lectures - he's an excellent communicator and advocate of the game. However, I once watched him play a match in a London tournament and saw him make a hurried and fairly obvious late game blunder. I overheard a spectator sniggering that he should practice what he preaches in his book.

It didn't cost him too badly and Chris went on to win his match, but it does raise an interesting point. No matter how well you know the theory, applying it under pressure will always be a challenge. Even the best players, like Chris, sometimes make blunders. There isn't a player in the world who doesn't make foolish mistakes from time to time; we're all human. Never be afraid to slow the game down. If you're feeling the pressure, pause, sip your drink and think about it. (I know that's easier said than done!)

TOP TIP 8: IT'S NEVER TOO EARLY TO THINK ABOUT DOUBLING

This next position shows a situation I was once in where I missed a double. My opponent (Black) started with a 4+3 and was immediately hit by my lucky throw of a 4+4. Black then threw a 6+5 so he was unable to re-enter. I was very optimistic about my chances, but I assumed that it was too early to think about doubling because I'd only rolled the dice once. But this was in fact clearly a double I should have offered and one that my opponent should have accepted. As it happened, I failed to offer the double. I went on to roll well but it was too late. I lost my market and ended up winning but missed the opportunity to double the stakes.

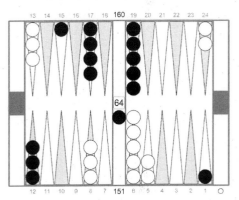

Even though it's early in the game, White should offer the doubling cube at this point.

TOP TIP 9: REMEMBER YOUR MISTAKES

Quite often we can be too busy congratulating ourselves after a game to notice that we missed a trick. Always look back and see what you could have done better. It's human nature to assume that we haven't really made mistakes on the days that we win. But hindsight can be a great tutor!

TOP TIP 10: DON'T PLAY FOR STAKES HIGHER
THAN YOU CAN AFFORD

The problem with playing for high stakes is twofold. Firstly, you become nervous and make mistakes. Secondly, you can't afford to accept or offer a cube when it is logical to do so. If you start a game but wouldn't be able to pay up if the cube was offered to you at 8 or 16, you are at a huge disadvantage. This would also make you afraid of offering an 8 or 16 cube; which is just as bad. If you are in over your head, after you lose a few points you start becoming far too timid with the cube, and you'll also start playing too carefully for fear of getting gammoned. You should avoid getting into a situation where you are playing for stakes you can't afford because it will affect your decisions and, in the long run, cost you a lot of money.

TOP TIP 11: ALWAYS TRY TO DO AS MANY GOOD THINGS
AS YOU CAN IN ONE MOVE

In the example on the right, you've thrown a 3+3. This is a very useful throw as you can do four good things with it. You can re-enter off the bar, you can hit Black, you can move a midmarker and you can make your own 5-point. You can't always do that many things with one throw, but always be looking to achieve more than one thing with each throw.

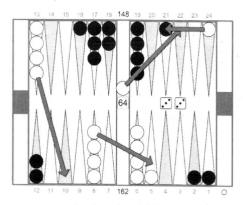

One throw; four good deeds.

And finally an important tip that an amazing number of players at every level forget:

TOP TIP 12: STOP WHINGEING!
NEVER COMPLAIN ABOUT THE DICE!

We've all played against someone who spends the whole game grumbling about the dice and, let's be honest, we've all done it ourselves at times. You should avoid doing this at all costs. Not only does it look bad, but it will also distract you from playing the best that you can. Complaining might have worked out occasionally for John McEnroe, but for the rest of us it is usually counterproductive.

Phil Simborg told me that there are five reasons why you should never complain about the dice:

1. It suggests your opponent is only winning because he is lucky and implies that he is not skillful. This is very bad form and insulting.

2. Nobody cares. Everyone is tired of hearing it. Everyone only sees their own bad rolls and forgets their great ones.

3. It's often not true that you are unlucky. If you think you are rolling more than your share of bad rolls, you're probably playing badly and not realizing it, because the worse you play, the more bad rolls there are and the more good rolls you give your opponent.

4. If you concentrate on your bad rolls, you will play worse. Complaining focuses your mind and energy on the *wrong things*. You think about how badly you are rolling, or how well your opponent is rolling, instead of what you really should be concentrating on: what is the right decision?

5. Complaining makes the game less enjoyable... for *you*. The more you make an issue of your bad luck, the more you will remember the bad luck and the less fun you will have playing, even if you win!

It's not fair!

Bob Hope... not looking so hopeful!

16

GIANT LAWS

It's often been said that you learn more
from losing than you do from winning.
I think, if you're wise, you learn from both.
You learn a lot from a loss.
It really gets your attention.

MORGAN WOOTTEN

At the Monaco World Championships in 2014, I was facing a good player in the first round when he found himself faced with a tricky situation (as shown below). Should he run or should he hit?

I could see that both options were good. Yet in my heart and in my gut I knew I wanted him to pass me by. I knew if he hit me I would get that sinking feeling. I was silently saying 'Please don't hit me' to myself, over and over, like a kid to the school bully. So what did he do? He hit me.

If he had been able to read my thoughts, he would have known what I didn't want him to do. We are not mind readers but we can still put

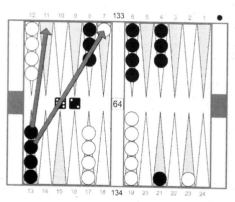

With his 6+2, my opponent had the choice whether or not to hit me.

ourselves in the shoes of our opponent for a moment and 'think what move would I hate most if I were him?' Once you know this, obviously this is the move you should make; the one that causes him the most pain! This is actually Simborg's Law, as explained below.

In this chapter, I am going to share with you some of the laws of the giants of the game that should, if you keep them in mind, help you win. Some of them you will recognize from the tips and tactics we've already covered.

LAW ONE: SIMBORG'S LAW

Simborg's Law states that **you should always make the move your opponent will hate the most**. It is a great discipline in helping you arrive at the correct move. If you are playing with the White checkers, it's tempting to play the entire game staring at those White checkers and thinking about what is happening with those White checkers without ever considering the game from Black's point of view. By looking at the board from your opponent's perspective, you'll be able to see clearer opportunities for the White checkers to create problems. You will start to understand the game and your position better. Simborg's Law tells you to consider the game from a new perspective. Once you've worked out which move will hurt your opponent most... play that move!

LAW TWO: WOOLSEY'S LAW

Woolsey's Law is very similar to Simborg's Law but is concerned exclusively with the doubling cube. Woolsey's Law states that, **when considering offering a double, always think first about how you would reply if you were in your opponent's shoes**.

So, when you are considering offering a double, try to work out which of the following your opponent is thinking as he considers accepting it.

If you think he's thinking 'Maybe', i.e. if you reckon he won't be certain either way, you should definitely offer the double. If he ends up declining and forfeiting the game, that's a good result for you, as it's a guaranteed win. You never know what might have happened. Your opponent may have thrown well enough next time to bring him back from the brink of the position that made you want to offer the double in the first place and gone on to take two points from you. If he ends up *not* accepting it, he may have made a mistake and gifted you a point.

Even if you weren't right to have offered the double, you must have been well in the lead to have considered offering it, so you've still doubled the stakes if he accepts while you're on top, which is no bad thing. Also, if you are not sure, maybe that's because it's a close decision. That's the perfect time to double. If it's close, you stand far too great a chance of losing your market when it's next your turn and would probably have to be content with playing without the double.

If you think he's thinking 'No', you should go ahead and offer the double and take the points you get when he declines, rather than playing on without the double (for much the same reasoning as above).

If you think he's thinking 'Yes', you might still want to consider the double but

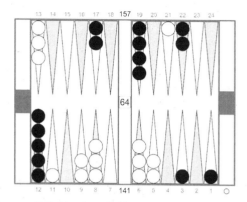

To double or not to double? Put yourself in Black's shoes to get your answer.

think carefully before doing so. There is only one reason to offer the doubling cube if you are sure your opponent is going to accept it, and that is if you are too likely to get to a position on the next roll where he is sure to pass because your position is too good, i.e. when you've missed your market and it becomes too late to offer the double.

On the left you are on roll (it is your turn), and you are wondering whether or not to double. In this position, ask yourself, 'If I were Black, would I accept the double or not?' If I was Black, my answer would be, 'I'm not sure.' Now, as White, you know for sure that you should double!

LAW THREE: O'HAGAN'S LAW

O'Hagan's Law follows on from Woolsey's Law in a way, and states that **if there is a 25% (or more) chance that you are going to lose your market, you should offer a double.** This is a brilliant way of determining whether it's time to double before it's too late.

You can calculate your chances of losing your market by looking at which throws would make your opponent decline the double on the next turn. Then deduct any poor throws that would greatly improve his position. If the total is 9 or more of the 36 possible throws (that's 25%) that would make him decline the double if you offered it next time, then it's time to offer that cube now!

On the right, it is quite difficult to determine whether you should double or not. But if we apply o'Hagan's Law, we can come up with an answer. If you do not offer the double now and you go on to roll a 6, there is no way that Black would accept the offer of the double

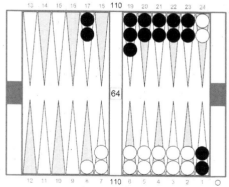

According to O'Hagan's Law, White should offer the double, but only just!

on your next turn; you will have lost your market. There are 11 ways to roll a 6, so there are 11 ways in which you would lose your market. But you also have a couple of rolls that are also so disastrous for you that we call them 'anti-market' losers. What if you rolled a 5+5 or a 4+4? Both would put Black into a very strong position. In total, you have 11 market losers, and 2 anti-market losers .This is a net total of 9, which, out of 36 moves, is 25%. So this position is *just* a position from which you should offer the double, according to O'Hagan's Law.

LAW FOUR: STICK'S LAW

Stick's Law will also help you with doubling decisions. This law states that **most normal situations where both players have built formidable primes (known as prime versus prime positions) are situations where a double should be offered and should be accepted.**

The position below looks pretty bad for Black as he is facing a full 6-point-prime. However, you (White) also have your two backmarkers stuck behind a strong 5-point-

prime, so there is light at the end of the tunnel for Black. Eventually you will have to break up some of your prime and he should be able to escape. That may well be before you are able to free your own backmarkers. This usually gives Black enough to accept a double if offered. In this position, he has a 30% chance of winning and with only one backmarker in your home board, it doesn't look like he has a very high risk of losing a gammon. This fits

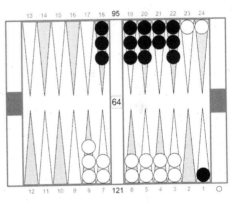

In this situation, you should offer the double and Black should take it.

Stick's description of 'normal'. In this situation, if you are smart enough to offer the double (as you should), Black should accept it.

LAW FIVE: THE 'RULE OF FOUR' LAW

This is another law that helps you make doubling decisions, although it's a little trickier to get to grips with. Basically, the 'Rule of Four' states that, *if* your opponent is holding

just your 5-point or bar-point *and*
you have four or less checkers on
your mid-point, *and* you are ahead
by 15% or more in the race, you
should offer a double. In most cases,
your opponent should accept it, but
might decline and forfeit the game
if the odds of getting the opportunity to hit you are too low and/or
your lead in the race is too great.

In this example, your position
meets the criteria of the 'Rule of
Four,' and you should offer the double.

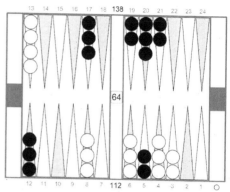

The Rule of Four Law.

LAW SIX: BALLARD'S LAW OF GAMMONS

The great player Nack Ballard invented the Law of Gammons, which states that if **you
don't think you'll lose a gammon, you should accept a double.** Basically, as long as
you're pretty sure you're not going to lose a gammon, you should accept what you consider
to be a reasonable cube offer whether or not you think you have a strong chance of
winning.

LAW SEVEN: SIMBORG'S FORGET-ABOUT-IT LAW

Phil Simborg's Forget-about-it Law states that **you shouldn't base your decision on a
similar situation that has occurred before.** For example, most situations in which you
find yourself considering a double will look very familiar. When you consider your best
option, it is all too easy to remember what happened the last time you were in this situation. Perhaps the previous time you doubled from this position and you ended up
leaving a blot that your opponent hit and you subsequently lost. Or maybe it was a race
where you had a comfortable lead and your opponent threw two doubles in a row and
went on to beat you.

In backgammon, as in life, if you dwell on the bad things that happened to you in the
past, you could miss golden opportunities that you will later regret. Don't let past expe-
riences give you cold feet and stop you from offering the doubling cube when your tactics
are telling you to do so. This could really hurt you, especially if it makes you offer the

cube too late, so that your opponent declines and you only win one point. As Albert Schweitzer once said, 'Happiness is nothing more than good health and a bad memory.' Don't let the fear of the freak occurrence or joker stop you from taking a decision that is statistically correct. Stick to your logical rational reasoning.

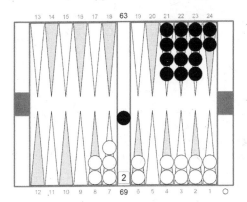

Offer the double regardless of whether it backfired
on you in a similar situation last time.

In the game above, you're going to win this game unless your opponent rolls a 5 together with a 4, 5 or 6. Okay, that's exactly what happened the last time you were in this situation, but... forget about that now and make the decision to offer the double because that is what your statistical knowledge tells you to do. Let go of the previous bad things that have happened to you in the game.

PART IV

WHERE & WHEN TO PLAY

Leo DiCaprio unwinds with a smoke and a game.

17

PLAYING
FOR REAL

No other game generates as much adrenaline.

CHRIS BRAY

You do meet some fantastic characters. Most people are very friendly in the backgammon community, but some keep themselves to themselves and don't really
get involved in conversation, giving monosyllabic answers in response to
questions.

I always try to make small talk. I will always ask my opponents where they are based and
which tournaments they've played in before. I congratulate them on a good play and so on.
Most players will come out of their shells and engage in conversation as long as you don't bother
them when they are trying to concentrate. Some are very chatty, like me.

I was once playing a long online match against an experienced player based in Florida and
half way through the match he asked to take a time out. When he returned he explained that
he had an argument with his girlfriend and they'd split up. He'd locked her out of his apartment
and while he'd been playing me, she'd been banging on the door. He'd paused the match to let
her back in and they'd kissed and made up, all in the time it took me to have a cup of tea whilst
waiting to resume the match.

◎

Live tournaments are not only fun, they are also great practice grounds. There's no better
way to sharpen your skills than to play under pressure. There are tournaments almost
everywhere. You will find plenty at local clubs; whether they are dedicated backgammon
clubs or other sports clubs holding occasional backgammon tournaments. You can search
for these online.

Then there are the more serious annual and professional tournaments. At the top
end there is the World Series of Backgammon, the World Championships in Monaco
and many major tournaments in the U.S., such as the Chicago Open, which is the most

famous and has also offers excellent lectures by professional players. Other famous international tournaments include the Japan Open and the Nordic Open.

If you are lucky enough to live in a big city, you will probably have many choices of tournaments. There are clubs all over London, including Crystal Palace, Ealing, Clapton and Fulham. There are also the traditional West End clubs like the RAC in Pall Mall, which, together with outliers such as the MCC (the home of cricket) and the Hurlingham club, form a league. And there is also a London Backgammon League of Individual Players. There is a fantastic list of hundreds of tournaments across the world at http://www. chicagopoint.com/calendar.html.

HOW DOES A TOURNAMENT WORK?

Tournaments are almost always knockouts, 'round robins,' or a combination of both. A round robin usually happens in the early stages of the tournament where a group will play each other for the right to get into the later rounds such as the quarter final. Tournaments sometimes have different categories for beginners, intermediates and experts. Don't let pride get in the way of you joining the right group; you will have more fun and learn more by playing opponents against whom you are well-matched.

Having said that, I can't see the point of having an intermediate tournament at the world championship. Who wants to say, 'I'm world champion at the intermediate level. So I'm the champ, apart from everybody who *didn't* put their name down as being mediocre.' I also can't see the point of having a lady's world championship tournament when the current overall world champion is female. And Akiko Yazawa is not the first female winner.

As Walter Trice says, 'In a backgammon match, anybody has a reasonable chance to beat anybody else. The player who doesn't respect his opponent is likely to get greedy, to take risks when he shouldn't and to fail to take risks when he should.'

A COUPLE OF MATCH PLAY AND TOURNAMENT RULES

Crawford and Jacoby were two giants of the game in the 60s and 70s. Together, they wrote a very useful book called *The Backgammon Book*. They dedicated it to 'the genius who invented the doubling cube and made backgammon the game it is.'

The Crawford Rule was invented by John Crawford in the 1960s and is now used by almost everyone when playing matches. **It is used exclusively in match play, not money play**.

Crawford, who was a great bridge player as well as a top backgammon player, ruled that, in a match being played for points rather than money, when one player is one point away from winning, no doubles are allowed for the next game.

For example if you are leading 4-1 in a match to five points, neither of you are able to double in the next game. This prevents the losing player from automatically doubling when there is no possible upside for the winning player in doing so. It protects the match leader from receiving a double when there is no value in doubling himself, so it makes the game fairer.

It's worth remembering this rule before you get to the late stages of a match because it can put you in a position where it is a long haul back, because not only are you losing against an opponent who is one away from winning but you also cannot double.

The Jacoby Rule was created by Oswald Jacoby and is conversely **only used in money play, not match play**. The Jacoby Rule states that if no doubles have been offered in a game then gammons and backgammons do not apply.

TOURNAMENT DICE

Many tournament players bring their own dice. These are precision dice, which are precisely manufactured making them less likely to be biased towards any number and therefore more likely to give random dice throws.

Above: Precision dice from the World Championships in Monaco – a snip at $35.
Left: Akiko Yazawa, 2014 World Champion

PLAYING TO YOUR STRENGTHS OR WEAKNESSES

The early rounds of tournaments are often matches played to just 5 points. This is, of course, brutally short, but there are some ways you can turn this to your advantage. If you are playing someone better than you, you should make the match short by ramping up the doubles. Conversely, if you think you are the superior player, stretch the match out so that you end up playing as many games as possible, making it less likely that you will be obliterated by a series of flukes.

Later rounds in tournaments are often to 9, 11, 17 or even more points. The longer the match, the more your skills and experience will persevere. When you're a novice it's fun to enter a small tournament where everybody has a shot at getting to five points. As your skills improve, you can play in the longer events.

Some tournaments auction their players to raise the value of the winning prizes; the 'owner' of the player shares a portion of the winnings. This is called a Swiss auction.

Doubling in tournaments is allowed but most apply the Crawford rule. So don't forget your automatic double and free drop in the game after a Crawford game.

A friend of mine played in a pro-am tournament at Crockford's Casino in London's Mayfair. He is a novice and was lucky enough to get paired with

Tournament auctions: as close as I'll ever get to becoming Miss Universe.

Falafel, the man many believe is one of the greatest players ever to pick up a pair of dice. Together they progressed as far as the semi-finals with my friend having only a passing understanding of what was going on. This seems like a fun way to learn about the game, a bit like learning how to drive with Lewis Hamilton behind the wheel!

WHAT IS A CHOUETTE
AND HOW DO YOU PLAY IN ONE?

A chouette is a game where one player plays against a group of players who play together. The winner of the game becomes the 'king of the mountain' in the next game and faces everyone else. It's great fun, generates an enormous amount of noise and is also a great way of learning the game at a more advanced level because the team members get to confer about their next move. Phil Simborg, who is considered the number one chouette player in the worlds says about the competitive tension of working as a team in a chouette, 'It toughens you up and prepares you for marriage.' Phil put his kids through college with his chouette winnings!

The word *chouette* is French for 'screeching owl', which indeed describes the sounds that can be heard emanating from a chouette. The game evolved from a sociable tournament known as a **Swiss Tournament**. This is a mini informal tournament between friends (maybe six to eight), a sociable occasion where everyone chucks a small amount of money into a pot, and either everybody plays everybody or there is a couple of rounds and then a final. The winner takes the pot.

As the character Mike McDermott says about gambling in the film *Rounders*, 'Listen, here's the thing, if you can't spot the sucker in your first half hour at the table, then *you* are the sucker.'

Phil Simborg, maybe the best chouette player in the world, and certainly the most experienced.

In a game of chouette, the single player on one side is known as the box. His 'opponent' can be any number of team players ruled by a captain. This obviously generates a lot of (often loud) debate. To keep the game moving, the captain makes all the moves without contradiction until the doubling cube comes into the game. Once the doubling cube is on '2', team members can chip in with their opinion, but the captain still has the final word if the team can't agree.

However, here's where it gets quite complicated.

Each member of the team has his own doubling cube and can use it whenever he likes against the box. Accordingly the box makes individual doubling decisions against each team member. As you can see, the box can be playing multiple cubes at the same time in the same game and can therefore win or lose a lot of money. It sounds confusing and at first, it is. But chouettes are great fun so if you get invited to one you should give it a whirl.

Different chouettes have different rules and standards of etiquette. However, what never changes is the feeling (when you are the box) that you are playing an opponent with a multiple personality! The pressure of this and of potentially playing for large amounts of money in a single game, can lead to some unusual plays. Whatever you do, don't play for big bucks until you've played many a chouette (unless your wallet is a bottomless pit!)

Even if a chouette does cost you some cash in the course of an evening, you will at least get your money's worth in terms of learning and having fun. And it will help you to get used to the pressure of playing under the scrutiny of an audience in a backgammon tournament. The ability to read people will help you in chouette. You can also benefit by observing everyone closely and noticing if someone is prone to making mistakes when playing under pressure, particularly when that player becomes the box player. You should also be aware, when you are captain, to know which of your team players are really worth listening to.

In many chouettes, when two players disagree strongly about a move, a bet on the play is often made. A picture is taken and at the earliest convenience the play is put into a computer program to determine the winner. The bragging rights are usually worth more than the bet! But everyone learns something from the experience.

Be careful if you are joining a chouette where everybody knows each other pretty well except for you. You will be at a disadvantage because the others all know each other's skills and styles. Chouettes are pretty commonplace in backgammon and wherever you play, if you ask your local club, it's likely that someone will know where there is a regular one that you can join. I highly recommend giving it a go. It can send your adrenaline levels off the charts but it will also turbocharge you along the learning curve.

Whether playing in a formal chouette or even just with a friend or a small group, it's always fun to play for money even if it's just for the price of a drink. It gives the game that competitive edge and tension. You don't have to play for an amount that can ruin an evening... or even a friendship!

Backgammon players,

Roger Low and Paul Magriel play blindfolded in a demonstration match with Denise Hemingway and George Plimpton (Backgammon Galore).

just like other gamblers, always remember the good times and are hazy about the number of times they have lost. One player I know claims to have won £4million over the years. I always wonder — as he reminds me of this — why I am paying for the drinks again!

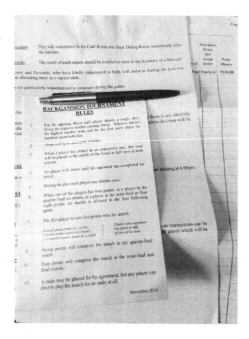

Remember to check the rules before you get going. They vary considerably, especially concerning player auctions.

LEARN FROM THE PROS

At many tournaments and backgammon club meetings there are matches between professionals that you can watch, or even lectures you can attend. You can even find videos of backgammon matches on YouTube. You can sit back and watch matches between many of the best players in the world. As you watch them play, think about what play or cube decision you would make. (You can even pause the video and make a decision and then press play again to see if you made the same decision as the pro.)

Unless you are a great player yourself, you will be surprised and even shocked at the number of moves you see played that you would never even have thought of. You will learn one of the most important lessons in life... that **you don't know what you don't know**. Watching the pros will show you how much you have to learn.

PLAYING BACKGAMMON ONLINE

Cheating in live backgammon games is difficult and, thankfully, rarely happens. But in online matches, where you can't see your opponent, it's much easier to be hoodwinked.

There's a great scene in the Bond film *Goldfinger* where Goldfinger employs Shirley

Eaton's character to look at his opponent's cards and transmit the news to her boss who is playing by the swimming pool below. (There's another story about this film that I love. Apparently Ian Fleming named his legendary villain Goldfinger after the architect Ernő Goldfinger, who had built a house too close to Fleming's. When Ernő threatened to take legal action about this, Fleming apparently offered to change the name of the villain to 'Goldprick'. Unsurprisingly, he never heard from Ernő again!)

What happened in the scene in the film could never happen in backgammon because there are no hidden aspects to the game. However, it is possible to cheat online. That's where cheats can and do prosper.

Shirley Eaton in 'Goldfinger'.

When I first caught the backgammon bug, I wanted to get as much experience as possible, so I started playing against other people online for money. I only played for small amounts but they started to add up, given the frequency at which I lost! One of the reasons I lost was that I wasn't very good, but the other reason was that my opponent would be sitting next to two screens: one showing his match against a sucker (that'll be me) and the other running his favourite computer software. He was fast enough to fool me. He would move the obvious moves himself and then update a replica game on computer programme while I was pondering my next clumsy move. On the more difficult moves or cube decisions, his computer would give him the answers. Ultimately, I was playing against a machine. I might as well have been playing Roger Federer at tennis for money! I discovered this the hard way after losing some money and a more seasoned player warning me not to play for money online. There are plenty of gambling sites and poker dens online where you can play backgammon for money, but it's a risky business. On the other hand, playing people online for fun is a great idea and a brilliant way of improving your game because you can play whenever you feel like it.

There are some good sites such as FIBS http://www.fibs.com/, Gammon site http://www.gammonsite.com/ and Backgammon Masters http://www.backgammonmasters.com but my favourite is where a lot of professionals play, Grid Gammon, although it is less easy to join as it is by invitation only: http://www.gridgammon.com/.

Rupert Hill — no relation (at least that's what I claim when he is being embarrassing, as in this story; at other times I acknowledge him as my brother) — had tried for some time to be accepted by 'Grid Gammon', the most exclusive site in online playing. He had started playing on the computer program Xtreme Gammon, where his results got him rated him as a 'casual player' (which is a polite way of saying that he was no good). Rupert took this term to mean that he had a reasonable grading as a player. When he couldn't get registered at Grid Gammon he emailed its administrators complaining that he should gain entry because he was rated as a 'casual player'. This is a bit like writing to Harvard to ask why your straight E-grades didn't get you a place.

Baron Vernon Ball plays Muhammad Ali in Puerto Rico in 1976.

Photograph by Maurice Barie

18

RAGE AGAINST
THE MACHINE

*I am able to calculate things effectively
and quickly. Like other areas of the game,
it can be improved with practice.*

BOB KOCA
(PH.D. MATHEMATICS PROFESSOR, BALTIMORE)

You can learn a great deal from playing against a computer, but beware of playing too much against the 'bots' and not enough in real life. Do try to play humans once in a while so that your tolerance threshold stays at normal levels. My friend Jamie Lee became so fixated on his quest to overcome his portable backgammon computer that he would play through the night. I would get a desperate phone call from him in the morning. 'Simon,' he would splutter. 'He's up 143 points to 109. How am I ever going to catch him?'

Another problem that will arise if you play too often on the computer at the expense of real-life games is that you don't get to practice your pip counting because it's always shown on the screen for you. When you come to play a live match you'll struggle to work out your pips in your head and know whether you are up or down in the race and by how much. This information is often essential to making the best checker and cube decisions. It's easy to get sucked into playing the bots for hours. They're perfectly behaved opponents: they never complain, they don't drip food or drink on your board, they don't cheat, and they never cough in your face.

Don't make the mistake of playing machines exclusively or you may find yourself behaving like that character in a Kingsley Amis book who is so used to being alone that she points her remote control at people when she wants to turn them off. If you haven't played against enough human beings, when you do, you might find yourself impatient when your opponent doesn't move instantly, incredulous when they make an unusual double or move, and intolerant when they count a move wrongly.

I do love playing backgammon with people but if you want to continue improving then a good computer program needs to be part of your practice as well.

WHAT'S THE BEST COMPUTER PROGRAM
TO USE AND HOW DOES IT WORK?

There are some very sophisticated computer programs on the market now. I've tested most of them and while I like the *Jellyfish*, *Snowie* and *Gnu* programs, my favourite to date, is *Extreme Gammon (XG)*. Many, if not all, professionals feel the same way — currently the XG program is streets ahead of its competitors. The reason for this is partly because the developer, Xavier Dufaure de Citres, is constantly updating and improving the product with direct help from several experts. *XG* is also the most reasonably priced, at around $60 (at the time of writing) compared to around $400 for *Snowie*, which was the popular favourite before *XG* came along a few years ago.

Computer programs emerged in the 1990s and changed the face of our understanding of the game. This is because the program can roll out the rest of the game from any given position or cube decision in a few seconds. It can then advise you what is the best move if you were playing from the same position. It can also show you if you make the wrong move and how that can affect the rest of the match. Unfortunately, these programs don't come right out and tell you why one move is better than another, but since they show you how many wins, gammons, and backgammons each move produces, with some practice and coaching you can usually derive enough insight from the numbers to come up with the right conclusions.

Doing a rollout is more fun than it sounds because you can get the computer to do all of this analysis while you're playing a match against it. And it can then point out to you if you've made a small mistake, which it calls an **error**, or a big one, which it calls a **blunder**. (If you tire of having this pointed out to you, you can turn this function off!) Many people play their matches and games against other humans on XG to save the trouble of having to input the game and positions later, because you can set the computer for two players to play each other. Also, if you play an online game against another player, your play can be automatically imported into your XG program for a full analysis of both your play and your opponent's. The downside to this is that you cannot kid yourself about how well you've played; there really is nowhere to hide!

Here's how to improve your game using a 'bot'.

Play a match against the program. And always play at 'world champion level'. Notice not only when you make a mistake, but also how your opponent is playing (he *is* the world champion, after all!) After the match take a look at the mistakes you've made (these are listed on the left-hand side) and think about what you might have done differently.

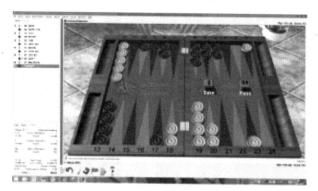

Figure 160: Left: XG in action.

Figure 160A: Left, below: The XG analysis column.

When you play a live match and you find an interesting position or cube decision, **take a note of it or even take a picture of it.** Back at home you can put this position into your program and it will tell you what it thinks you should have done. You can learn a great deal from this.

Not only can the program tell you the best move, it can also list all the other moves you could make and how wrong they are. If you've offered a double but it was the wrong decision, the computer will let you know by how many percentage points you were wrong to do so.

Don't forget to download the **phone or tablet version** of your program. The iPhone version of XG is fantastic. You can start sneaking in games when you are on the bus, in the dentist's waiting room, or in the airport departure lounge.

XG also carries many features that will help you to understand the game. There are advanced tools for match play, including match equity tables, take points and gammon values, racing formulas, and dice distribution analysis that quickly shows how every possible roll would play from a given position. This program also maintains detailed running statistics so you can get an overview of your game and even see trends and tendencies in cube and checker play to guide you towards specific areas of your game that could use improvement. It's like holding a magnifying mirror up to your face so you can see all your blemishes! But if you are serious about improving your game, this tool is a must. How can you improve if you don't first identify your weaknesses?

Some people feel that the bots are biased. I have a friend who plays against XG and feels that if he doesn't take the program's advice on making a particular move it often 'punishes' him by giving him some nasty luck on the next roll. This shows how skewed our thinking can be when playing this devious game. The dice on XG and all the other respectable programs are totally random. As

Great while waiting for root canal surgery.

Phil Simborg, a major player in the development and marketing of XG says, 'If we wanted to make XG cheat, we would make it cheat in favour of the player, not against him. We would rather people love the program and recommend it than curse it and trash it!'

Playing against the bots regularly gives you a wonderful dose of harsh reality. You are playing the equivalent of Mochy or Paul Magriel every time. You are likely to lose a lot. Your cube decisions will be relentlessly criticised. However, if you can't take the heat, you can set the bot to play you at a much lower level and it will intentionally make a lot of mistakes. This will be more like playing mere mortals!

This type of practice will undoubtedly help you to improve your game. At the end of each match, the program will tell you how you played. A perfect rating is zero: i.e. your opponent plays at zero level if you set your computer to world champion level. It's a bit like golf; the higher the number, the worse your rating. Anybody who plays below a rating of 5 consistently is playing at a professional standard, and below 10 is extremely good. Anybody can, of course, play at a rating of 0 over one game if it goes well, but that howler of a game they play next can give them a rating of over 20 in another game. Your long-term average will obviously improve the more good games you play.

Kit Woolsey, one of the great players of the modern era, regularly plays a full match to 11 points against *XG*. He then takes time to analyse all of his moves and mistakes. John O'Hagan, another backgammon great, plays a match to 13 points every day.

Mochy, the No. 1 Giant in recent years, started a club to register players who can play live, recorded matches and play under a player rating of 4 (a 4.0 PR, the player rating that is shown on the computer). After one year, only six people had qualified. There are probably less than 50 people in the world who could qualify for the 'Under 4 PR Club' and maybe 500

The great Kit Woolsey

who could consistently play under 6 PR. However, if you go to an online server and record matches, there are many playing under 2 PR. You might ask yourself how that could be possible without the aid of a bot, and you will have asked a very good question. The answer is that many of them are playing with the help of XG or another bot!

Although it's not as romantic nor as much fun as playing human beings, you will improve markedly if you play regularly like some of the world's best players do, especially if you play in 'tutor mode', displaying all your mistakes as you go along.

These computers really do have the answers as to what is the best move because they are 'neuro-nets' which means that they constantly improve their performance by learning from experience tens of thousands of times. In a way, all of the thinking behind our checker and cube play is really a series of **stories we tell ourselves** to explain what is, these days, scientifically proven by the computers.

ALWAYS SET THE MACHINE TO WORLD CHAMPION LEVEL

If you had the chance to play – for fun, rather than money – either against the world champion or a beginner, which would you choose? In boxing you might prefer to take on the novice. But in backgammon the answer is always to take on the champ and see how you get on. This is even more appropriate when playing against the computer for two reasons: firstly because if you win you really are achieving something and not kidding yourself into thinking you're good by winning against the program's beginner level. If you play against the computer on its 'beginner' setting, it can make hilariously poor moves.

But the most important reason always to play against the computer on its 'world champion' setting is because every time you play, as well as noting your own moves, you will have a masterclass from an expert. You'll be playing against a brilliantly ruthless machine whose every move you can watch and learn from. At times it will do things that might surprise you; at this point you can take a step back and try to figure out why it has made a particular move. Every great move you witness is an excellent learning opportunity.

KEEP A SIX OFF YOUR CARD

There used to be a column in the *Sunday Express* (and I am showing my age here) called *Keep a Six Off Your Card*. It was a weekly prize for amateur golfers who could play a round of golf without shooting more than a 5 on any hole This is not nearly as easy as it sounds because most amateurs will have a bad couple of holes, even if they do well on most of them. If you manage it, it's considered a highly acceptable round and you'll be seen as one to beat.

You can apply the 'keep a six off your card' challenge to backgammon. When you're playing against *XG*, you can go wrong in three categories: 'error', 'blunder' and 'huge blunder'. If you can play a match and avoiding making any huge blunders and even any blunders (i.e. keeping all blunders off your proverbial card), you will be playing at a very high standard indeed. I do not believe it is possible to play a match of reasonable length either against a human being *or* a machine without making some errors.

Keep a six off your card.

As soon as you start making blunders you will lose matches far more frequently against good players and if you also make huge blunders you will be taken to the cleaners. But if you don't worry too much about the errors, think hard about each move and just try to avoid those blunders you will be amazed at your results; your whole game will improve.

Think of it this way. The perfect backgammon player (i.e. a computer) will play at a PR of 0. The best human beings in the world will play, on average, at a PR of between 2 and 4. If you avoid blunders in a match you will be playing to a PR of around 10. If you make blunders you might be playing to a PR as low as 20 or 25. If you are playing, on average, at a PR of 10 and you face a professional who is playing at a PR of around 7, the difference between your PRs is only 3. If you are playing that same professional and you are playing at a PR of 25, the difference jumps to 18. If you're only a few PR levels worse than your opponent, you have a chance of winning, even over quite a long match (there is enough of a luck factor to make up for the difference). But if there is a massive gap between your ratings, you will struggle to beat him.

PLAYING HUMAN BEINGS

Can we humans play better than the best rollout computers like XG? The answer is yes and no.

No human could calculate the moves and percentages of a backgammon game as accurately and fast as a computer. On the other hand, the computer has one weakness:

it always assumes it is playing another computer, or a player as good as a computer. The computer doesn't account for normal human error. .

Knowing the strengths and weaknesses of your opponent can give you an edge that the computers simply don't have. For example, many beginners fall into patterns of flawed play that are easily spotted. You should familiarize some of these.

The most obvious beginner traits are as follows.

There is the **cautious player** who doesn't take risks and will often go to great lengths to avoid an exchange of hitting with his opponent.

Then there is the **overly aggressive player** who always hits. You can set traps for him by leaving blots exposed where he really shouldn't hit.

Conversely there is the **extra timid player** who almost never hits, even when he should.

There's also **the player who cuts and runs** because he's losing in the race, when he should really stay and fight.

There are also players who will **automatically reject a double** if they are losing the game, even if mathematical logic says they should accept it. You can gain big equity over a period of time against a player who does this.

On the flip side of that coin, some inexperienced players will **almost always accept a double** just because they want to see how the game turns out. Even some very good players do this, including apparently one former world champion, as I previously mentioned. I won't name him, but he is the only world champion featured in this book wearing sunglasses!

Just like in poker, there are players who have 'tells'. They will tell you with their body language whether they are going to accept or decline before you offer them the double. If you are in a money session, some players get very conservative when they are ahead for the day and drop just about every game when offered the cube. These same players become 'steamers' when they are losing, taking wild chances in an attempt to turn the match around. Of course, these approaches will tend to accomplish just the opposite of their what they intended to achieve, especially if the players' opponents notice and learn how to exploit their weaknesses.

If you're playing very good tournament players they are well aware of these pitfalls and will be trying to avoid these mistakes, but if you're playing friends or at your club, or with other people online, you will start to see the players who have some of these bad habits. Currently the bots don't account for these weaknesses as they assume they are playing against the best. Maybe artificial intelligence will, one day, learn to factor in human behaviour!

UNDERSTAND WHY YOU ARE MAKING A MOVE

In 1918, Max Planck won the Nobel Prize for physics and went on a tour giving talks from town to town. His chauffeur boasted to him that he knew the talk off by heart and so at one town it was agreed that the chauffeur would give the talk and Max Planck would watch from the audience. This plan went swimmingly well and the talk was very well received, until somebody from the audience asked a technical question. Quick as a flash the chauffeur replied: 'that's such an easy question that I'm going to let my chauffeur, who is in the audience, answer it.' The point here is that it's not enough to learn by rote dozens of good moves from playing repeatedly against a computer. You need to understand why you are making the moves, so that you can adapt to the millions of other situations that will come up. In other words, a true understanding of the subject rather than a parrot-fashion repeating of moves will make all the difference.

Darling, why on earth would you take that double?

Tina Turner in September 1979

©Las Vegas Backgammon magazine

19

NEXT MOVES

I'm often asked 'Is there any magic to getting good at backgammon?'
My answer is yes.
There are two magic ingredients:
Study and Practice.

BILL ROBERTIE
(TWO-TIME WORLD CHAMPION)

PLAY AND TAKE NOTE...

I was once playing a difficult match at my local tennis club when I faced a crucial cube decision. As I took the decision, I thought I'd got it wrong but I wasn't sure. Phil Simborg always says it's best to take a picture of the position with your phone and then feed it into your XG program later, to see what you should have done. Unlike Phil, I care too much about how I look. I always feel that taking a snap of the position would look nerdy and foolish in the middle of a sociable evening, so I can never bring myself to do it. Instead, on this occasion I took an old envelope out of my pocket and scribbled some notes on it about the position. This was unusually diligent of me and I felt rather pleased with myself as I tucked the scrap of paper away. At many tournaments nowadays, you will see players record their entire match and analyse it later. I'm not sure I like that idea myself, but I can't fault people for working on their game.

A few days after this match, I took my dog Hector out for a walk and he did what dogs are supposed to do on a walk; he made a deposit on the pavement. I reached into my jacket pocket for a little plastic bag but, alas, I had none left. I looked around nervously to see if I could get away with walking off (a fairly serious crime in my part of London). I noticed that Yvonne — an elderly and respectable neighbour — was about a hundred yards behind us. She's a nice lady but has an eye like a hawk; there was no way she hadn't seen Hector do his business. She was closing in on us and I was left with no choice; I had to do the right thing. The only thing in my pocket was the old envelope on which I had written my backgammon notes. I had no choice but to use it to scoop up Hector's mess. I should've taken Phil's advice and taken a picture!

The dog ate my homework.

There's a big difference between playing casually with your mind elsewhere, and playing to improve. Einstein's definition of insanity is doing the same thing over and over again, and expecting a different result. So do take notes and pictures, look up positions on your computer or in your backgammon books when you get home, even ask a friend, but don't walk away from a match or position that you've made a bad decision on none the wiser. Ask yourself: do you want 20 years of accumulated experience or one year of experience repeated 20 times (which is what happens to most players who don't attempt to evolve their understanding of the game)?

READ ALL ABOUT IT

There are many books about backgammon that can help you. Unfortunately, many of the advanced and specialist ones are out of print or hard to get hold of, such as *Backgammon Bootcamp* by Walter Trice and Jake Jacobs and their enig-matically titled *Can a Fish Taste Twice as Good?* which is excellent on the science of playing varying levels of opponent as well as being full of fun and interesting anecdotes about the game.

For these I recommend some of the specialist backgam-mon websites such as Backgammon Galore http://www.bkgm.com/ and the Backgammon and Board Games Shop: http://www.bgshop.com/index.htm.

Can a Fish Taste Twice as Good?

The British player and author Chris Bray has written a number of good books including **Backgammon to Win** and **Backgammon for Dummies**, both of which are very sound. Some of the great players of the 70s have left a legacy of good solid books. I particularly recommend *Backgammon* by Paul Magriel and *The Backgammon Book* by Jacoby and Crawford. There are quite a few other similar — if not quite as comprehensive — books from this era.

Spookily, quite a few of these books have the same snappy title.

I strongly recommend, after you've finish reading this book, reading the books of Bill Robertie. Bill has written three very good backgammon books. *Backgammon for Winners*, *501 Essential Backgammon Problems* and *Backgammon for Serious Players*. All of these are excellent for intermediate players and include well-explained scenarios from one of the best backgammon brains around.

Backgammon for Serious Players is a step-by-step account of five matches featuring top players along with Bill's commentary.

READ ONLINE ARTICLES

There are also some excellent online resources. Paul Magriel, two-time world champion, used to write a column for the New York Times. You can read a backlist of his articles at http://www.bkgm.com/articles/Magriel/NYTimes/indexByDate.html. At Backgammon Galore you can also read a lot of other useful backgammon articles: http://www.bkgm.com/.

There are also many good pieces at Chicago Point http://www.chicagopoint.com and at the official US Backgammon Federation site at http://usbgf.org/ where they have a regular magazine called *Primetime*. These and many other sites are all worth dipping into and they generally also have blogs that you can get involved with as well.

If you join the USBGF, which is a leading membership-based authority, you will find yourself a large online resource, including many video lessons from members. For example, you can watch hundreds of short videos made by Phil Simborg, which cover virtually every area of the game.

PRACTICE AGAINST THE COMPUTER

Kit Woolsey and John O'Hagan practice every day but fellow Giant Ed O'Laughlin goes further and reports that he plays against the computer and studies his errors for approximately 12 hours a day, 6 days a week!

Although it's not as romantic or as much fun as playing human beings, you will get better if you play regularly in the same way as Kit, John and Ed do. Especially if you play in tutor mode. One criticism of the computers is that they tell you *what* is right but not *why* it is right. **It is in the figuring out *why* a move is good that you gain true knowledge and skill.** I have to admit that the 'why' is often elusive, and that is where you can get great help from a teacher or mentor.

Kit Woolsey – who practices relentlessly

PLAY AGAINST REAL PEOPLE ONLINE

Playing online can be great fun and also has the advantage that you can do it at the drop of a hat. You don't need to arrange anything in advance and you can play for as long or as short a time as you wish. As previously discussed, don't play for money against someone you can't see. If you feel like being that reckless with your cash, at least find a good charity to give it to, and play people online for fun.

You can always capture a moment in an online game by taking a picture or screen grabbing it on your computer. This is excellent for studying moves afterwards and feeding the position into your game software.

TRY USING THE CHAT FACILITY WHILE PLAYING

Some players can be hilarious to talk to, and it gives you more of a 'live' match feel.

TAKE LESSONS

Taking lessons is really easy these days because you can play against a professional online as well as in person. Local clubs will often have members who offer lessons. Phil Simborg has established BackgammonLearningCenter.com and has brought on several other teachers who specialize in beginners, intermediate, and advanced lessons, as well as teachers who provide backgammon lessons in Spanish, German, and French. Many of Phil's students have gone on to win major tournaments around the world.

In summary, to help you take your game to the next level: **play**, **read**, **play people online**, **play against computers**, and **take lessons**. If you do an assortment of these you will not only stay fresh and interested, but you will also accelerate your learning and progress. Although if you do all of them you may not have time to lead a sane, normal life... just like many a backgammon professional!

One thing is clear (and this applies to any skilful endeavour), you need to get good information or help from books, articles, videos, teachers, mentors, and bots, and then you need to put in hours of study and practice, particularly what is called 'deliberate practice,' actively questioning your moves and attempting to improve at the same time. Studies of top athletes, chess players, and people who have become champions in any game or sport prove that all of these people have one thing in common: **they worked hard and they worked smart**.

John Huston and Paul Newman between takes.

20

THE LIFE IN
THE GAME
AND THE GAME
IN LIFE

*Avoiding danger is no safer
in the long run than outright exposure.
Life is either a daring adventure, or nothing.*

HELEN KELLER

I t's amazing how many parallels there are between the two known worlds: Planet Earth and Planet Backgammon. And here are 25 observations that apply in both.

I recently took part in a match to qualify for selection to the UK backgammon team. The winner would join the team for the 2015 European Championship in Budapest, playing for his country, something I never imagined possible. The loser would slink home with nothing.

I faced Neil Smith, a well-known and able player. During our chat before the match Neil mentioned that he wrote computer programs for banks. My heart sank – 'not another boffin'. We had to play a match to 15 points and Neil made a flying start, winning a gammon on a two point game to go ahead by 4–0, helped by a few good throws, and then doing it again, so that within 20 minutes of the start I was losing 8–0.

I fell into some very negative thinking: my mind raced, thinking that if this carried on and I lost 15–0, it would be a humiliating rout and I would never be considered for international selection again; I would look ridiculous; and why did I even think I could play someone of Neil's calibre? I was an imposter and had been found out. I never wanted to try to play at this level again. I was a loser.

I wrenched my focus back on to the matter at hand, and as so often can happen in backgammon, the luck started to turn around and soon I stopped ranting to myself as some hope emerged. Suddenly I couldn't throw a bad pair of dice, and two gruelling hours later I was leading 14–10. Neil hauled a few points back until it was double match point (match point to both of us). I held my breath…and I was over the line. Somehow, I had qualified for the UK team and would play in the European Championships.

◎

Which leads me to the first of our 25 observations:

1) Keep your focus on the things that concern you

2) You can't control events but you can choose your reaction to them

Vanderlei Cordeiro de Lima is a Brazilian long-distance runner. His career peaked during the 2004 Athens Olympics marathon. To win the marathon in Greece, the birthplace of the Olympics, where the race actually starts in the town of Marathon, is a supreme prize for a long-distance runner. De Lima was leading more than three quarters of the way around when an Irish priest called Neil Horan, who was protesting that the end of the world was nigh, pushed him off the track and into the crowd. De Lima lost valuable time and was overtaken. He continued the race and ended up with a bronze medal.

De Lima being pushed off the track.

To me, De Lima is a hero; not just because he carried on with the race, but because of his attitude. As he came down the home straight to achieve third place, he danced a jig, smiled and waved to the crowd; an astonishing reaction from a man who could rightly claim to have been robbed of a gold medal.

He never won an Olympic gold but he was voted Brazilian sportsperson of the year and continues to be renowned for his supremely sporting reaction. In fact, he is perhaps more famous today for this than if he had won gold. Being sporting and philosophical about losing has had its own rewards.

3) If you believe you are unlucky, you will be unlucky

Watch out for that 'I'm having terrible luck' feeling. It creeps up on you and then every move seems to fit your theory. But it's just an illusion. If you make a bad move and are punished because of it, suddenly you feel unlucky for the rest of the match.

My friend Alistair Reynette-James is convinced that, whenever we are together, I have good luck and he has terrible luck. He believes this is true whether we're playing backgammon or visiting a casino. I think he's turned this feeling into a self-fulfilling prophecy. As the match goes on he proves himself right time and time again. Beware of this attitude; it will sap your confidence when you most need it.

When you focus on your bad luck, not only will you play worse because you assume you won't roll well, but – win or lose – the game will be less enjoyable.

4) Never gamble for stakes higher than you can afford

This applies to all areas of life. I will never forget when I had my first big gambling loss having to walk several miles home from a casino in the early hours with my heart in my boots because I couldn't afford the cab fare. The sinking feeling after a loss is always stronger than the euphoric feeling after a big win; they are not two sides of the same coin. If you can't afford to take a 64 cube, don't sit down to the game in the first place.

5) Curiosity can be expensive

Most people accept doubles when they shouldn't just because they have an insatiable curiosity and need to know how the game is going to turn out. This will often cost them a lot of money. Don't worry if you've done this, it's a human mistake that we've all made. Nobody likes to walk away from a game without knowing if they would have won, but sometimes you have to. In life, too, you can't always know all the answers.

6) When our luck is good it's 'our right' and when it's bad it's 'not fair'

This is another psychological trick that your mind can play on you, not only in backgammon but also in many other areas of life. I was once at the end of a very close match and I was losing slightly. Then I threw a 6+6 and it gave me a chance. But then my opponent also threw a 6+6 and won. I felt like I'd had rotten luck, but that's absurd; I was losing and then we have both had the exact same luck. You have to recognise this skewed thinking for what it is.

7) It's not the cards you're dealt it's how you play them

If the dice don't go your way, focus on making the right move rather thinking about the terrible luck you've had and wishing you had better dice. In the long run, luck is meaningless and over thousands of games it doesn't exist; the statistics even out. In life, too, when things don't work out the way you'd hoped they would, make the best of what you've got. As the old saying goes, 'When life gives you lemons, make lemonade.'

8) Practice makes perfect

In his book, *Outliers: The Story of Success*, author Malcolm Gladwell says, 'Practice isn't the thing you do once you're good. It's the thing you do that makes you good.' Whether you are the Beatles, Michael Jordan or just a backgammon player trying to lose less, if you steadfastly follow his rule that it takes 10,000 hours of practice to become an expert at anything, you will eventually achieve what you want.

9) There's always another game

So get over it. Whatever's gone wrong, in life or in backgammon, when it doesn't work out for you try to remember there are other opportunities. Adopt a 'plenty more fish in the sea' kind of attitude. And remember, over time, tragedy always turns into comedy. You will eventually laugh about the setbacks that seem so disastrous now.

10) Almost always, if in doubt make the more positive play

In life and in backgammon, be brave. If you can see something's a bad idea, don't do it. But if you're fairly sure it's a good one but has risks, and you're afraid of it then, 'Feel the fear and do it anyway!' Most of us play too timidly most of the time. You don't want to end up regretting the things in life that you didn't do. Y. H. Jackson Brown, Jr. said, 'Be bold and courageous. When you look back on your life, you'll regret the things you didn't do more than the ones you did.'

11) Be in the game. It's all about creating equity

By creating equity I mean creating a possibility that something can be achieved even if the percentage chances are low. Sometimes you play great and lose; sometimes you play fantastically and still take a thrashing. That's just life... and backgammon. You won't catch any fish unless your bait is in the water. And the more often your bait is there, the more fish you will catch. Playing matches, having a go, being in the game, creates equity. So, too, in life when you go for that scholarship, apply for that job, ask that person you think is out of your league out on a date, you take a calculated risk. You know that sometimes it's not going to pay off, but in the long run each time you go for something in life, you are creating equity that adds up. And when it does pay off, it feels fantastic! If you don't try, nothing will happen.

12) Play the man not just the game

Many players seem to believe you should play the same game no matter who your opponent is. However, I think it's worth taking into account that most human beings are... well... human! If your opponent is playing terribly, would you be more or less likely to accept a double early in the game? The answer is that you should accept more doubles, and for two reasons. Firstly because he is likely to offer you a double too early, which makes it a take for you. Secondly, even if his double is correct, if you are a better player, you have lots of chances to out play him and go on to win the game, even if the odds are technically against you. Of course, you also gain control of the cube, which, against a lesser player, is very valuable. In life, too, it never hurts to tailor our approach to the person you're dealing with!

13) Sometimes it's better to be wrong but 'wromantic'

In the classic spoof history book *1066 and All That*, it is suggested that the Cavaliers in the English Civil War were 'wrong but wromantic' and the Roundheads were 'right but repulsive'. Sometimes it's better to be a Cavalier. If you are playing somebody for fun who is a very basic player it's so tempting to wipe the floor with them, offer doubles when you know they are going to be confused, and generally be ruthless. But it's no fun cracking a nut with a sledgehammer. I would err on the side of mercy, especially if you want to enjoy playing them again.

14) Keep an eye on the little details

Sometimes, when you only have a 1 or a 2 left to play in your move, you can feel your opponent's impatience as you spend time thinking about it. But these small moves — deciding where to slot, whether to split, or where to leave a shot — are the backbone of your game. Neglect these details at your peril. Let's say one play is only 10% worse than another, so you don't worry about studying it and getting it right, well, make 10 of those 10% worse plays in a game and you have thrown away a game! As in life, it is often the smaller details that can make all the difference... look after the pennies and the pounds will take care of themselves.

15) Everybody thinks they are better than they are

Apparently 85% of us believe we are above average car drivers, which, of course, doesn't add up. In the same way, backgammon players who have reached a reasonable standard generally believe they are rather better than they really are. I know I do! (One player I know takes good advantage of this. She often acts rather dizzily in setting up the pieces at the start of a match and can get confused as to where some of the counters go. Then, when she is offered a double early in the match that really shouldn't have even been considered from a player who thinks he's better than he is, she casually accepts, giving him a false sense of security. She then plays faultlessly while it gradually dawns on her opponent that he's been hustled!) A little humility will always serve you well in life.

16) You learn more from losing than winning

In the 1950 Football World Cup, England lost to the USA... who were novices. Everybody thought it was a disaster for English football. England was the birthplace of the modern game and had millions of fans, while 'soccer' as the Americans call it, was a lesser-known game in the U.S. Who benefited most? Who thought about the match and what went wrong afterwards? Almost certainly it was the losing team, England (although it took them another four World Cups before they won the trophy). We should all use our defeats and analyse them. But we shouldn't forget to analyse the games we've won as well.

17) Avoid making snap decisions

At least once per game, if you play a move quickly, when you look back and analyse it, you will find that you missed a better play. The fastest player I know is Ben Goldsmith. Ben always races through his moves. I sometimes don't know how he does it. But for most of us, when we slow the game down and take it easy, we will play much better. Some players have been known to take a full 10 minutes over a move, which can obviously frustrate the opponent. All I'm suggesting is that you take at least 10 seconds as your minimum time. When you see a great move take those few moments to look again at the position and check it really is the best move. If you do this are guaranteed to win more. Remember: more haste, less speed!

18) Stay in the moment

Take every move as it comes, don't steam ahead because you've just lost three games in a row, or because your opponent just threw a double 6 twice in a row, just take each position on its own merits. Surprisingly few people can stay in the moment in life, but you will achieve more if you can do it.

19) Trust your instinct

In his book *Blink*, Malcolm Gladwell explains how, in that first moment of receiving new information your subconscious comes to a judgement. The rational mind then takes over and analyses whatever is on the agenda and often comes to a different decision. We've all experienced the regret of not following our hunches. The same applies in backgammon. More often that not, your first instinct is right. Should you take those 10 seconds I suggested, to look for all other possible moves? Or should you go with your first instinct? The answer is, you should do both. Take the time to analyse the move but always remember what your first instinct was when you saw the position. Trust your instinct in the end.

20) Hindsight isn't always a wonderful thing

You can do the right thing in backgammon and still get punished for it. This unpredictability is one of the reasons we love the game. If you make a move that is correct but it doesn't work out for you, it makes no sense to beat yourself up for it or wish you'd done something differently. You know that if you played that same move 10,000 times it would have paid off for you most of the time so don't let the mind trick you about this. The same is true in life of course. Sometimes you make the right decision but you get a rotten outcome, but do this often enough and statistically you will come good in the long run.

21) Identify what you really want to do

Have you ever had a difficult decision to make and decided to toss a coin? I find this can be a great way of revealing what you *really* think is the right choice. You decide which choice heads and tails will dictate and then you toss the coin. When the coin lands and you see the result, you usually instantly feel either regret or relief. This reveals your real gut feeling; you should go with that and not the coin toss result. I'm not suggesting you toss a coin in the middle of a backgammon match, but learn to trust your gut feeling because it's probably right.

22) Watch out for that steam

When you lose your composure in backgammon, it's called 'steaming'. Perhaps you've lost a game or two with some rotten luck and you start to feel that life is unfair. Then you start to feel the dice are constantly against you. Indignant, your blood rises. You start accepting and offering doubles that you shouldn't. You begin to play recklessly. You're 'steaming'. I'm sure you've done this plenty of times in life, too. But in both backgammon and in life, try not to lose your cool like this. If you do feel the steam rising, try not to let it influence your decision-making. This is easier said than done, but recognising when you're starting to approach this state is half the battle. Conversely, however, you can take advantage of your opponent's lack of self-control. When you notice him starting to steam you'll know some cheap points are likely to be up for grabs! Backgammon champion Malcolm Davis says, 'I try really hard not to pay any attention to luck but when I'm playing an opponent who's getting aggravated and upset about his luck, then he's not going to play at his best.'

23) Don't 'snowplough' your children

Backgammon is a brilliant game for children and there are lots of great reasons why you should teach kids how to play. They'll learn a lot competing socially, about luck and sportsmanship, and it can help them with mathematics. But don't make the mistake of 'snowploughing' them as I did. This expression comes from Clarissa Farr, headmistress of St Paul's Girls' School in London who caused a stir in the media when she warned against 'parenting with a snowplough.' This, she explained, is 'clearing everything away in front of the child so that nothing can go wrong.' This will not prepare them for life, because life always throws up obstacles to the best-laid plans. I found myself doing this when playing my son, Teddy. I would let him try a move again when he had blundered, warning him about pitfalls and generally trying to stoke his interest by boosting his confidence. When I tried to get him interested in playing against the *XG* software to boost his game so that we could have more competitive matches together, he looked aghast and said, 'But I already beat you all the time anyway, Dad.'

24) Don't judge a move by its result

It is all too easy to judge whether you've done the right thing by whether it works out for you. You make a move or take a risk and it works out well and it is only natural to file that away in your mind as the right move to have made, causing you to repeat this move over and over again whether it was right or wrong. If you need to check a backgammon move after a match, have a look on the computer which will show you what would have happened had you played the same move thousands of times, thus letting you know whether it was the right one. A solitary outcome, good or bad, is not enough data on which to base all of your future decisions when placed in similar situations.

25) Be kind and be polite

Not only will the game, as in life, be more enjoyable, if you have gracious manners at the table, but your opponents and other people will treat you better as well. And good things will happen to you along the way, so it's not only the best way to behave, it's the smart thing to do.

Winning is only half of it.
Having fun is the other half.

BUM PHILLIPS

And finally, remember to HAVE FUN *along the way!*

In both life and in backgammon, remember, like Henry here, to HAVE FUN.

ABC director Henry Watson jumped into the Las Vegas Dunes hotel pool to win a $300 bet at the world amateur backgammon championships in 1982.

Index

G

H

J

K

L

M

Pirates

DUDLEY SCHOOLS
LIBRARY SERVICE

CAPTAIN
PUGWASH
and the PIGWIG

Schools Library and Information Services

S00000726965

Also available: